SURVIVAL QUEST

VOLUME ONE

STUDENT EDITION

Authors

SHARON R. BERRY, Ph.D., and OLLIE E. GIBBS, Ed.D.

LifeWay®

CHRISTIAN SCHOOL RESOURCES

Biblical Solutions for Life

Biblical Solutions for Life

Published by
LifeWay Christian School Resources
One LifeWay Plaza
Nashville, TN 37234-0182

Created and Developed by

Christian Academic Publications and Services, Inc.
Birmingham, Alabama

ISBN: 0-7673-9338-4
Dewey Decimal Classification: 248.82
Subject Heading: TEENAGERS \ CHRISTIAN LIFE \ BIBLE--TEXTS

SurvivalQuest, Volume One: Student Edition

Printed in the United States of America

For ordering or inquiries visit *www.lifeway.com,* or write LifeWay Church Resources Customer Service, One LifeWay Plaza, Nashville, TN 37234-0113

SurvivalQuest

Table of Contents

INTRODUCTION

Surviving and Thriving

Stress, hurt, anxiety, frustrations, anger, disappointments, depression, bewilderment, crisis, panic. Life is tough. And it's getting tougher for young teens. What can you do? Give up? Go hide in a cave? Sit in a corner and suck your thumb?

You are about to study a 36-week course entitled *SurvivalQuest*. You will learn practical, down-to-earth skills based on Biblical examples and principles. Beyond surviving the upsets of life, you will learn to thrive as you develop relationships and build toward your future. Perhaps no other study could be more important to you at this time of life.

Do bad things happen to young teens? They surely do. Students at the high school in Paducah, Kentucky, found this out when a classmate opened fire on a group meeting for prayer. Ben Strong, a 17-year-old, spoke these words at his friends' funeral: "They died for what they believed in. It hurts to see them go, but to them, there was no better way. They were praying. As soon as they said, 'amen,' they saw the face of God."

A few months later a similar incident occurred in a middle school in Jonesboro, Arkansas. A 13-year-old and an 11-year-old opened fire on their classmates and teachers who had exited Westside School for a false fire alarm. After murdering four classmates and a teacher, the two have nothing to look forward to except to lie on their cots and cry for their mothers. The motivation for such devastation? The older boy's girlfriend had broken up with him.

In listening to the media coverage of these events, we share the anguish and grief of families and friends suffering the loss of loved ones. Our hearts ache for students who couldn't solve their deep emotional conflicts in more positive and productive ways. We are left with the questions: How could such a thing happen, and how can it be prevented in the future?

More quietly and with less fanfare, 1.5 million teens a year attempt suicide feeling that they have nothing to live for or that their mistakes are so grievous, they cannot face the future. Other teens turn to gangs, sex or crime seeking a way to ease their deep hurts and satisfy the longings of their hearts.

There are better ways to resolve the conflicts and hurts. Without making light of the problems you face, your study of *SurvivalQuest* will provide you with choices and solutions. You will learn to accept your natural emotions and desires as you exercise options toward recovery and growth. You will learn not only to survive but thrive in the midst of your circumstances.

Throughout your study you will be drawn back to the characteristics of God, who made you and loves you. Knowing He is sovereign—in control of all events and their outcomes—can give you the confidence to face tomorrow. When you feel that there is no hope, no way out of the pit, God can magnificently step into your life to bring peace and sureness of the future (Jeremiah 31:3–4; 29:11).

> ". . . Yes, I have loved you with an everlasting love; therefore with loving-kindness I have drawn you. Again I will build you. . . . For I know the thoughts that I think toward you . . . thoughts of peace and not of evil, to give you a future and a hope ."

Nobody messes up too much for God. No one is beyond His power to forgive and restore. Having extensively persecuted early Christian believers and assented to the death of Stephen, the Apostle Paul called himself the worst of sinners. Arrogant, prideful, self-centered and self-sufficient, Paul was a wreck, yet God could bring victory and joy to his life. After becoming a believer, Paul's life was no flower garden. The Christians distrusted him. The Jews hated him, stoned him and left him for dead. He suffered disappointing friendships, imprisonment, shipwreck, poor health—you name it. But in the end, Paul wrote the song of the overcomer (Romans 8:28, 31–32, 37).

"And we know that all things work together for good to those who love God, to those who are the called according to His purpose. . . . If God is for us, who can be against us? He who did not spare his own Son, but delivered Him up for us all, how shall He not with Him also freely give us all things? Yet in all these things we are more than conquerors through Him who loved us."

We can overcome. We can survive. And we can thrive. But to do so, we must follow the same foundational steps as Paul. As you read each step, consider whether you have honestly taken this step in your own life. God's way or no way, the choice is yours.

1. Recognize God as the source of all goodness and happiness in this life and the life to come. With Him, all things are possible. Without Him, nothing is. Because He is life, light and love, He alone has the wisdom to provide clear direction for your life, the power to help and the love to forgive.

2. Realize your own helplessness. We are made of clay and a few trace minerals. We have a mindset that is in opposition to God. The Bible says that we have deceitful hearts, determined to wickedness. Given our best efforts and best intents, we fall miserably short of God's standard. This failure is called sin. The solution is to agree that, in ourselves, we have no answers. Therefore, we come to God in confession of sin and the helpless condition of our lives.

3. Receive Christ as Savior. God's method of forgiving sin and establishing a right relationship with Him is through His Son, Jesus Christ. By faith, we accept God's provision and make a commitment to live as He commands. In return, God sends the Holy Spirit to eternally live within us, giving us the desire and ability to live as God wants.

4. Reflect the relationship you have with God. Commit to learning all you can about God through Bible reading, prayer and interaction with other believers. Apply what you learn to the everyday experiences of life. Trust that in every situation, God is in control. His plan is bigger than we can see. It ultimately leads to building our character and conforming us to be more like Christ.

5. Rejoice in all things. Because God has a purpose and the final outcome is certain, you don't have to sweat the small stuff. Even in the most difficult trials and embarrassing mistakes, you can experience hope, peace and joy. Every circumstance can be your teacher toward spiritual maturity and successful living. Embrace life with enthusiasm as you grow up in Him.

These five steps can set the course of your life. They can make you emotionally secure and confident as you face the challenges of the future. They give you what psychologists call "resilience." This is the ability to rebound from life's upsets. It is the ability to regain composure in the midst of turmoil. It is the ability to rebuild after the most devastating blows imaginable. It is a key factor in "emotional intelligence" or an EQ that is recognized as being of far greater importance than IQ, intelligence, when considering success in life.

Begin with these five steps firmly established as your goals for life. Then as you study a different Bible person each week, along with the challenges they survived, apply the principles to the various ups and downs you face. When you complete the course, you will have learned how to both survive and thrive at life. You will be an overcomer.

> ". . . they shall walk with Me in white, for they are worthy. He who overcomes shall be clothed in white garments, and I will not blot out his name from the Book of Life; but I will confess his name before My Father and before His angels" (Revelation 3:4–5).

INQUIRY–ACTION I.1

SURVEY ON CHALLENGES AND CONCERNS

ITEM	RANKING OF CONCERN

	EXTREMELY HIGH										LITTLE OR NONE
	10 9 8 7 6 5 4 3 2 1 0										
	10 9 8 7 6 5 4 3 2 1 0										
	10 9 8 7 6 5 4 3 2 1 0										
	10 9 8 7 6 5 4 3 2 1 0										
	10 9 8 7 6 5 4 3 2 1 0										
	10 9 8 7 6 5 4 3 2 1 0										
	10 9 8 7 6 5 4 3 2 1 0										
	10 9 8 7 6 5 4 3 2 1 0										
	10 9 8 7 6 5 4 3 2 1 0										

INQUIRY–ACTION 1.1 (CONTINUED)

LETTER TO MYSELF

Based on the personal challenges and concerns I face, some things I would like to learn in this course are:

_____

_____

_____

In order to really learn and apply Biblical solutions to life problems, I make the following promises to God and myself.

☐   I promise to work on my relationship with God.

☐   I promise to study Biblical principles and apply them to my life.

☐   I promise to pray and be sensitive to the Holy Spirit working in me.

☐   I promise to seek godly counsel when I am in situations that seem overwhelming.

☐   I promise to help others find godly solutions to the problems they face.

Signature: _____

Date: _____

INQUIRY-ACTION 1.2

ROMANS 8

1. Throughout the passage we see a dramatic contrast in trying to live the human way versus living by God's Spirit. In the two columns below write words from the passage that describe these two ways to live.

The Human Way

_____

_____

_____

_____

_____

_____

The Way of God's Spirit

_____

_____

_____

_____

_____

_____

2. Based on your descriptions, which way of thinking would be best if you were facing a serious crisis? Why? _____

_____

3. Check verses 1 and 9 and explain how a person can change from a natural way of thinking to a spiritual way of thinking. _____

_____

4. Check verse 15. The term "Abba, Father" is very intimate and endearing. It's the picture of a little child who has climbed into his dad's lap, given him a big hug and said, "You're my sweet papa." As an adopted child of God, what special protections and privileges do you have? Name at least three based on the passage.

_____

_____

_____

INQUIRY-ACTION I.2 (CONTINUED)

5. Check verse 28. God has a big plan and can see the end from the beginning. Some things that seem so bad now turn out to be a blessing later. In hindsight, you can see how God was protecting you or working things to your eventual good. Write one example of this from your personal experience.

_____

_____

6. Check verses 35 through 39. Paul wrote a long list of things that cannot separate us from God then said, "Nor any other thing." Think about the challenges or problems students face. Can any of them separate you from God? Why or why not?

_____

_____

7. Check verse 37. Being more than a conqueror is an interesting idea. If you win, you are a conqueror. But how can you be more than a conqueror? Write at least two sentences to explain your ideas.

_____

_____

_____

8. Below are five principles based on Romans 8. Write the numerals 1 through 5 in the circles next to them to show their order in the Scripture.

◯ Tough times don't have to overwhelm us. We can overcome them through His love and power.

◯ Even in tough times, God has a purpose and a plan to bless us and make the eventual outcome good.

◯ Tough times cannot separate us from God's love and the future glory we will share with Him.

◯ Doing things man's way (the natural way) is opposed to doing things God's way.

◯ Christians are God's children and can be directed by His Spirit living in them.

INQUIRY-ACTION I.3

ROMANS 8:18, 28, 31B, 35 AND 37

Use the word bank to help you write the verses from memory.

according	God	or	those
against	good	peril	through
all	glory	persecution	time
and	Him	present	to
are	His	purpose	together
be	I	revealed	tribulation
called	if	separate	us
can	in	shall	we
Christ	is	sufferings	with
compared	know	sword	which
conquerors	love	than	who
consider	loved	that	work
distress	more	the	worthy
famine	nakedness	these	yet
for	not	things	
from	of	this	

ADAM AND EVE

Surviving Temptation

Have you ever seen a summer vacation brochure advertising "a beautiful getaway home at the base of Mount St. Helens volcano"? Are there any families that you know who would like to live on a houseboat just a few feet above Niagara Falls? Do you know of anyone who would be willing to buy a home that straddles the San Andreas fault? Would you be willing to take a swim in the Amazon River near a school of piranhas? Or, if you had a daughter, would you let her date a convicted murderer?

Some things just don't make sense at all—like lighting a match to see if your gas tank is empty. Or picking up a rattlesnake to see if it has been de-fanged. Matter of fact, if you knew anyone who did these things, you would probably call him just plain "stupid."

And yet there are Christians who flirt with risks far greater than any of these. That's right! They put themselves in the path of danger on a regular basis. They know that what they are doing will destroy them, but they are always willing to take the risk one more time.

Who are these people? They are the ones who place themselves in the path of temptation, knowing that they are unprepared to resist. Although God's Word has warned them about the dangers, they take the risk anyway.

Over the course of the last 24 hours, you have probably encountered some type of temptation. For a moment, think about that last time you were tempted. Did the temptation catch you "off guard," or did you willingly allow yourself to be tempted? Is this a temptation you've faced before? Did you resist, or did you give in to the temptation?

Temptation did not originate with God. James 1:13 says, "Let no one say when he is tempted, 'I am tempted by God': for God cannot be tempted by evil, nor does He Himself tempt anyone." Temptation originated with Satan. It was his strategy to lead us into sin. It was a strategy first used with Adam and Eve, and it has been used with each person who has ever lived—including Christ Himself.

The story of Adam and Eve (Genesis 3) is a familiar one. Adam had been instructed not to eat of the tree of the knowledge of good and evil (Genesis 2:17). Eve, according to Genesis 3:2–3, also knew that God had forbidden them to eat of the fruit. Yet, when Satan came to Eve, he told her: "You will not surely die. For God knows that in the day you eat of it your eyes will be opened, and you will be like God, knowing good and evil" (Genesis 3:4–5).

These words became the temptation that caused Eve to turn her back on God and believe Satan. Why did these words have such a powerful influence on Eve? Was it her desire for the forbidden fruit that resulted in her disobedience? Certainly not!

Understanding what it means to be tempted helps us to know the real reason Adam and Eve made the wrong moral choice. Temptation is an enticement or invitation to sin, with the implied promise of benefit to be gained from choosing the path of disobedience. In other words, temptation occurs when you believe that, in spite of your disobedience , you will gain something of benefit or pleasure. In the act of disobedience you have called God a liar and have chosen self above God.

Have you ever felt as if your parents or teachers were always picking on you? Maybe you have heard warnings or reminders like the following: "You had better get started on your assignment or it will never be finished on time." "I'm sorry. You didn't follow the directions; you will have to do it over again." "Don't forget, you promised to . . . ." Well, you get the picture.

Sometimes you may feel that the adults in your life have nothing better to do than sit around and think of things for you to do. Their purpose seems to be to "take all the fun out of life" as they devise ways to make you miserable. However, their warnings and reminders are not meant to make your life difficult. Actually, if heeded, they will bring happiness and peace to your life.

Charles Spurgeon, one of England's greatest preachers, once described the important "warnings" contained in God's Word. Using Psalm 19:11 as his text, Spurgeon explained why it is important for us to read and study the Bible: It warns us . . .

> . . . of the nature and danger of sin.
> . . . of our duties to God and our fellowman.
> . . . of the temptations in the world where we live.

Although we may not always understand, warnings and reminders are meant to protect us. Since God knows us and has only our best interests in mind, He desires to warn us of the temptation strategies that Satan will use.

According to 1 John 2:16, Satan's strategies for tempting us fall into three categories: the lust of the flesh, the lust of the eyes, and the pride of life. These strategies have been used by Satan since the time of the Garden of Eden. They are strategies that he still effectively employs today.

If you are human (and you know you are!), you are facing temptation in your life today. As you already know, temptation is real. Just as temptation is real, so is the ability to overcome it.

Consider the following "facts" about temptation:

Fact One: God does not tempt us, Satan does (James 1:13).

Fact Two: We are instructed to resist temptation (James 4:7–8).

Fact Three: God will give us the ability to resist temptation (1 Corinthians 10:13; 2 Peter 2:9).

Fact Four: We are to pray for deliverance from temptation (Matthew 6:13; Luke 11:4).

Even the sinless Jesus, Lord of the universe, was subjected to temptation (Hebrews 4:15–16). Although He was tempted, just like we are, He overcame the temptation. That is why it is so important to heed His warning in Mark 14:38: "Watch and pray, lest you enter into temptation. The spirit indeed is willing, but the flesh is weak."

It is because He faced temptation and was victorious over it that we can come to Him now. The words of Jesus are clear: Watch and pray.

Watch
• Be aware of Satan's strategies.
• Stay away from situations and people that would contribute to the temptation.

Pray
• Maintain a close relationship with the Lord.
• Openly confess your struggles and ask the Lord for the strength to resist.
• Seek prayer support from those who love you.

The challenge of temptation is a daily battle that you will face for the rest of your life. You can survive and be victorious if you determine to heed the words of Jesus to watch and pray.

INQUIRY-ACTION 1.1

TEMPTATION OR SIN?

Noted below are examples of both temptations and sins. See how many examples you can add to the list provided.

Examples of Temptation	Examples of Sin
1. a student's locker left open	1. taking someone's wallet
2. money on a desk and no one around	2. spreading misinformation about another person's character
3. seeing answers on another student's test	3. using profanity
4. _____	4. _____
5. _____	5. _____
6. _____	6. _____
7. _____	7. _____
8. _____	8. _____
9. _____	9. _____
10. _____	10. _____

What is the difference between a temptation and a sin? _____

_____

_____

INQUIRY-ACTION 1.1 (CONTINUED)

The definition of temptation includes two important phrases: "implied benefit to be obtained" and "path of disobedience." As you identify temptations that are real to you, also identify the "implied benefit" and the "path of disobedience." The first example has been provided for you.

	Temptation	Implied Benefit to Be Obtained	Path of Disobedience
1.	to cheat on a test	I'll get a better grade.	stealing / dishonesty
2.			
3.			
4.			
5.			
6.			

INQUIRY-ACTION 1.2

"JUST THE FACTS!"

Investigate "Just the Facts" surrounding the story of Jesus' temptation, found in Matthew 4:1–11.

1. Why do you believe the devil tempted Jesus?

_____

_____

2. What was the physical and mental state of Jesus at the time?

_____

_____

3. What was the devil's strategy for each of the temptations?

_____

_____

_____

_____

4. What did Jesus do each time?

_____

_____

5. What happened after the devil left? Why?

_____

_____

INQUIRY-ACTION 1.2 (CONTINUED)

Return to your definition of temptation. Note the two significant phrases in the definition: "implied benefit to be obtained" and "path of disobedience."

Suppose Jesus had not resisted the devil's temptations. What would the "implied benefit" and "path of disobedience" be for Jesus?

Complete the following chart by noting Jesus' temptation and the "implied benefit" and "path of disobedience" that would have characterized Him if He had yielded to the temptation.

	Jesus' Temptation	Implied Benefit to Be Obtained	Path of Disobedience
1.			
2.			
3.			

Inquiry-Action 1.3

Means to an End

✦ **1 Peter 5:8–9; Luke 22:31–32** We should recognize that Satan

_____.

✦ **2 Corinthians 11:14–15; 2 Thessalonians 2:9–10** Sometimes Satan
_____. That's the reason
some things seem so good at first, only later proved to be very wrong.

✦ **Luke 22:3–4; John 13:2** Satan put it into Judas' heart to _____.
Judas was motivated by money and power; this caused him to be open to Satan's
attack.

✦ **Proverbs 1:10** Satan can use others to _____
_____.

✦ **1 Corinthians 7:5** Satan can tempt us through our _____
_____.

Some people think that Satan is a powerful, monstrous being and they live in fear
that he will attack them. In reality, he is a paper tiger and has no power against
a Christian. Jesus said, "He (God's Spirit) who is in you is greater than he (Satan)
who is in the world" (1 John 4:4). You have no need to fear Satan. In fact, every
time you overcome a temptation, you prove to yourself and others that with
Christ, you can do all things.

INQUIRY-ACTION 1.3 (CONTINUED)

THE DEVIL ~~MADE~~ DIDN'T MAKE ME DO IT!

While Satan initiates temptation in the world, someone else initiates it in your own heart. Check the references and fill in the blanks to summarize your findings.

✦ **James 1:13** It isn't _____ because He _____

_____ .

✦ **James 1:14** It is _____ because he or she is

_____ .

✦ **2 Chronicles 21:1, 17** Even though _____ enticed him to disobey God, _____ accepted complete personal responsibility for _____ .
He did not offer the excuse, "The devil made me do it."

✦ **Romans 7:18–19** Just as we all do, _____ struggled with _____ .

INQUIRY-ACTION 1.3 (CONTINUED)

So, here's the situation: Temptations and opportunities to sin are all around us. You can blame Satan for that. But the real problem is that our heart desires connect to the opportunities before us. Thus, we must learn how to manage our heart desires. Complete these suggestions:

◆ *Matthew 4:4, 7, 10* Know and use God's Word to _____

_____ .

◆ *Matthew 6: 13; 26:41* Watch and pray so that _____

_____ .

◆ *1 Thessalonians 5:22; 1 Corinthians 15:33* _____ situa-

tions and people that _____ .

◆ *James 4:7* Grow closer to _____ ; resist and flee _____ ,

then _____ .

◆ *Ephesians 6:10–11* Develop self-control as you _____

_____ .

INQUIRY-ACTION 1.4

1 CORINTHIANS 10:13

𝒜 – ℬ	𝒞 – ℱ	𝒢 – 𝒵

INQUIRY-ACTION 1.4 (CONTINUED)

1 CORINTHIANS 10:13

M – R	T – V	W – Z

BARNABAS

Surviving Broken Relationships

There are many "laws" in nature. For example, there is the law of thermodynamics, Newton's second law and the law of conservation. Certainly the most well-known of nature's laws is the law of gravity. This is a law that you become painfully aware of whenever you jump over a hurdle, throw a ball into the air or lose your balance.

Have you ever heard of the law of echoes? The law of echoes may not be an "official" law of nature, but it does exist. An echo occurs as a result of terrain that allows one's voice to be repeated. It is common to hear an echo in a mountainous area.

The story is told of a young boy who loved to visit his grandparents each summer because they lived high on top of a mountain. He would often go out in front of their house, cup his hands around his mouth and shout, "HELLO!" Immediately, the echo of his voice would return, "HELLO . . . HELLO . . . HELLO." This fascinated the boy. He would spend hours shouting at the top of his lungs just to hear his voice in return.

One day the boy seriously misbehaved and his grandparents had to discipline him. As he went running out of the house, he screamed, "I HATE YOU!"

Much to his amazement, the surrounding mountainside responded, "I HATE YOU . . . I HATE YOU . . . I HATE YOU!" Upon hearing his own words repeated to him, he realized how very wrong he had been.

Isn't this just the way it is in life? We get from others exactly what we give to them. The law of echoes certainly applies to our relationships with others.

This point was very clearly made to Mrs. Pollard's eighth grade English class when she asked her students to write the names of all the people they didn't like. Some students could think of only one or two individuals, while others compiled a lengthy list.

She then collected the papers and tabulated the results. When she reported her findings to the class, the students sat in silence. From their own lists, Mrs. Pollard showed the students that those who disliked the most people were themselves the most widely disliked. The results were startling proof of the proverb, "To have friends, a man must show himself friendly."

Their relationships with their friends also proved the law of echoes. If you don't want your friends to gossip about you, you should not gossip about them. If you want to be treated kindly, be kind to others. Those who smile receive smiles in return. Those who use harsh words are spoken to harshly. What you deposit in the echo bank, you draw in return. And, sometimes, you'll get it back with interest!!

Too often, we are inclined to take our relationships with others for granted. We think that our friends, parents and other family members will always feel the same way about us. Unfortunately, things sometimes happen that cause our relationships to be broken.

Barnabas probably never thought that his relationship with the Apostle Paul could be broken. They both had accepted Jesus Christ as Savior and had dedicated themselves to doing His Will. They had worked together to establish the church in Antioch. They had even led the first missionary journey to spread the Gospel to other cities. But as a result of their disagreement over John Mark, they parted company and went their separate ways.

Broken relationships are a natural part of life. Sometimes, as was the case with Barnabas and Paul, they are caused by disagreements. But a disagreement is only one of many potential causes for broken relationships.

It is important to remember that the causes for broken relationships fit into one of two categories: "Causes We Have Control Over" or "Causes We Have No Control Over." Let's take a look at an example of each.

Good friends usually enjoy sharing personal and confidential information with each other. This ability to confide in one another and discuss things of personal importance, without telling anyone else, is an important part of a close relationship.

What happens when one of the friends violates the confidence and shares the private information with others? The trust between the two friends is lost, the feelings of one friend are hurt and the relationship is broken. Emotions of disappointment and grief, even anger and resentment, occur when a close friend betrays a confidence or chooses a different companion. The cause of this broken relationship could have been prevented if the information between the two friends had been kept private. The other friend had control over whether or not to share the confidential information with others.

Broken relationships also occur as a result of things over which we have no control. Chances are you have already experienced a broken relationship as a result of you, or your friend, moving to another city. Although you can keep in touch by mail, e-mail or telephone, it just isn't the same as doing things and going places together. The same sense of loss occurs when a good friend moves away as when the relationship is broken because of betrayal.

Since broken relationships are a natural part of life, how should you respond when they occur? The answer is not a simple one, but the following guidelines will be helpful.

Guideline One: Identify the cause.

This is the first and most important step. If the broken relationship is the result of something over which you had no control, it will help to write what you believe happened. If the broken relationship could have been prevented, identify what you could have done. Be sure to honestly describe your responsibility in the broken relationship.

Guideline Two: Seek God's direction.

Before you take another step, pray. Ask for God to give you wisdom as you seek to restore this relationship. Confess any wrongdoing on your part. Be honest with the Lord about your feelings and your motives. Ask the Lord to help you first to have a relationship with Him, then to have wisdom in your relationships with others.

Guideline Three: Wait on the Lord.

If a relationship was broken by someone else or circumstances over which you had no control, you often cannot fix the problem. It hurts, but accept that God must work in others' lives first. Don't retaliate because of your own hurt and anger. Continue to be kind and pray for God to help them.

Guideline Four: Acknowledge your part.

If the broken relationship occurred because of your actions and you have identified your responsibility, then seek God's forgiveness and acknowledge to the individuals involved your part in the broken relationship. This may be the hardest part because it means saying "I'm sorry" and really meaning it.

Guideline Five: Initiate "bridge-building."

Someone has to take the first step to restore a relationship. If you are responsible, that someone should be you! Determine how and when you will take that first step to put the past behind you and build an even stronger relationship in the future.

Although it is still a long time until Christmas, it is never too early to give the gift of friendship. Consider how each of the following can help you establish, restore and maintain strong relationships:

Seek out a forgotten friend.
Forgive an enemy.
Be patient with an angry person.
Express appreciation.
Do the dishes for the family.
Pray for someone who you know is hurting.
Encourage an older person.
Give your teacher a break—be especially cooperative!

Remember, the Lord promises to be the restorer of broken walls (Isaiah 58:12).

INQUIRY-ACTION 2.1

"SNAPSHOTS" OF BARNABAS

Individually, or in groups, look up each of the passages of Scripture from the book of Acts. Each passage gives you a "snapshot" about the life of Barnabas. Describe the "snapshot" you see in the space provided.

A Levite named Joseph from Cyprus (which means Son of Encouragement)

Acts 4:36

People who owned lands or houses sold them to put the money on the apostle's feet and distributed it to those who needed the money

Acts 4:34–35, 37

Barnabas told the disciples tha Soul was indeed one of the disciple

Acts 9:26–27

Barnabas was a good man, full of the Holy Spirit and faith, and a great number of people were brought to the Lord.

Acts 11:21–24

Barnabas went to Taurus to look for Soul and taught there for a year

Acts 11:25–26

INQUIRY-ACTION 2.1 (CONTINUED)

Set apart
for me Barnabas
and Saul for the
work to which
I have called
them

Acts 13:2–3

They set up
execution
and expelled Paul
and Barnabas
from their
region

Acts 13:42–43, 49–50

Paul and Barnabas
were chased off
by bulls and
wreath because
of their
preaching.

Acts 14:11–15

Barnabas and
Paul told about
the miraculous
signs and
wonders God
had done among
the Gentiles
throug them

Acts 15:12–13

Barnabas and
Paul had a
disagreement
and parted.

Acts 15:36–40

INQUIRY-ACTION 2.2

REASONS FOR BROKEN RELATIONSHIPS

1. _____

_____

2. _____

_____

3. _____

_____

4. _____

_____

5. _____

_____

INQUIRY-ACTION 2.2 (CONTINUED)

6. _____

_____

7. _____

_____

8. _____

_____

9. _____

_____

10. _____

_____

INQUIRY–ACTION 2.3

RESPONDING TO BROKEN RELATIONSHIPS
FLOWCHART

1 A relationship is broken.

2 Pray.

→ A _____

B _____

C _____

3 Determine what happened. Do you have personal responsibility?

Yes.

A _____

B _____

C _____

D _____

4 Don't involve others.

no.

A _____

B _____

C _____

D _____

E _____

INQUIRY-ACTION 2.4

COLOSSIANS 3:12–14

Translate the foreign language into Colossians 3:12–14.

TAT EOG HAB POTM KHML;

BWOA AFOA IA HACAA EACFY

SYAMD. BRATT POL WIT BOP.

_____

_____

_____

_____

_____

_____

_____

JOSHUA

Surviving Poor Decisions

Before you read this chapter, carefully consider the following question: "What is the most important principle that guides the decisions you make?"

Whether you realize it, or even want to admit it, the decisions you make each day are guided by what you believe to be most important in your life. If you are guided by the right principles, the decisions you make will be good ones. If not, you are doomed to making poor decisions. Jim Elliot knew the difference.

As a freshman at Wheaton College in Illinois, he wrote the following principle that was to guide the decisions he would make for the rest of his life:

"He is no fool who gives what he cannot keep to gain what he cannot lose."

This principle was based upon Mark 8:36: "For what shall it profit a man, if he shall gain the whole world, and lose his own soul?"

Jim has often been described as the "All-American Boy." He had a keen mind, a love of the outdoors, excellent athletic abilities and a passion for God. At Wheaton College he quickly became a top student as well as one of the most competitive members of the school's wrestling team.

During his time in college, he made a brief missionary trip to Mexico. As a result of that trip, God placed within his heart a burning desire to be a missionary. From that point on, his entire focus was upon preparing himself to serve God as a missionary. He made sure that the classes he selected and the organizations he belonged to would help him reach his goal.

Jim Elliot graduated with highest honors from Wheaton in 1949. After a year working and teaching Bible school in Portland, Oregon, he went to a ten-week missionary
training program at the University of Oklahoma. There Jim learned about the
Aucas, a tribe of Indians in Ecuador that was untouched by civilization. Jim immediately was inspired to go to the South American country and try to make contact
with the Aucas.

During the next three years, Jim prepared to go to Ecuador. Not only did he have to
raise the necessary financial support, but he also needed to prepare for his marriage
to Elizabeth, his college sweetheart. They arrived in Ecuador in 1952 and were married in 1953. Eighteen months later their daughter was born.

In January 1956, Jim Elliot finally made contact with the Aucas. He and five com-
panions flew into the area where the natives lived. That was the last time they
would ever be heard from again.

For six years Jim had prepared himself to take the Gospel to this tribe. Upon their
arrival, all six men were killed. In just a few moments of time, the preparation,
planning and prayers of six years had come to an abrupt end.

Your first response to this true story might be, "Jim Elliot shouldn't have gone there
to begin with. He made a poor decision." However, Jim Elliot's decision was a direct
result of the principle he had chosen to guide his life: "He is no fool who gives what
he cannot keep to gain what he cannot lose." From the beginning, he was willing to
give his life so that others might have the opportunity of eternal life. Although it is
difficult to understand why Jim Elliot had to die in such a tragic way, his decision
was anything but a poor one.

Poor decisions are made when we are guided by the wrong principles. The story of
Israel and the twelve spies (Numbers 13–14) is a perfect example. Once Moses had
led the people out of Egypt, they traveled to Kadesh Barnea. At Kadesh Barnea
Moses selected twelve spies (one from each of the twelve tribes) to go into the
Promised Land. Their task was to gather information and report back to Moses.

After 40 days of searching the land, the spies returned. Ten of the spies reported that the inhabitants of the land were like "giants" (Numbers 13:32–33). They were convinced that Israel would be destroyed if the people tried to enter the land.

Two of the spies, Joshua and Caleb, disagreed (Numbers 13:30). "Let us go up and possess it. . ." they said. Since God had promised the land to them, they knew He would give them the victory. But the nation of Israel listened to the ten spies and decided that they were unable to take the land (Numbers 14:1–3). Although God had delivered Israel safely from Egypt and provided for them in the desert, they would not trust Him to enable them to occupy the land He had promised to them.

As a result of Israel's decision, the nation spent the next 40 years wandering in the desert. Because of their unbelief, they would die in the wilderness. Only Joshua, Caleb and those under 20 years of age would be allowed to enter the Promised Land.

The principle that guided Joshua and Caleb's decision was very different from the principle that guided the decision of the other ten spies. Joshua and Caleb believed God's promise that He would give them the land. The ten spies believed that the inhabitants of the land were too powerful for Israel to defeat. Both decisions were guided by principle. However, the different principles led to very different decisions. The only way to avoid a poor decision is to be sure that you are guided by the right principle.

Sometimes you may feel that it is difficult to know what is the right decision to make. Remember, God is not playing "hide and seek" with you. He has not secretly hidden somewhere the "right" decisions for you to discover. Instead He is a God of revelation and wants you to know and do what is best for His kingdom and your personal life.

However, God does not treat us as puppets. His Word is not like a detailed road map that shows us every turn to make. It is more like a compass that gives us the direction toward which our lives are to be pointed. As you read God's Word, look for principles that you can use to guide your future decisions. By following the principles that God has outlined in His Word, we can be assured of making good decisions.

38

INQUIRY-ACTION 3.1

THE WILDERNESS WANDERINGS

I. The Three Stages of the Wilderness Wanderings:

Stage 1: Egypt to Mt. Sinai - 1 year

Stage 2: At Kadesh - spies sent into Canaan... wandered for 38 years

Stage 3: Final Moments Before Moses' Death

II. The Report of the Spies:

A. 12 spies were sent out to see if Israel could possess the land

B. The mission lasted 40 days, the land wash lush and productive

1. Ten spies report was "we are not able to go up against the people

2. 2 spies - Lets go up and take the land

3. Vote "We don't go"

INQUIRY-ACTION 3.1 (CONTINUED)

III. God's Response to Their Unbelief and Poor Decisions

A. This is the 10th time the people had rebelled

B. Their bodies would fall in the wilderness

C. No one over the age of 20 except Joshua and Caleb would enter the Promised Land

D. They would wander for 40 years 1 year for everyday the spies were in Canaan

E. The majority report leaders would die of a plague

INQUIRY-ACTION 3.2

THE DECISION-MAKING CYCLE

Actions based on God's Word, prayer and godly counsel from others:

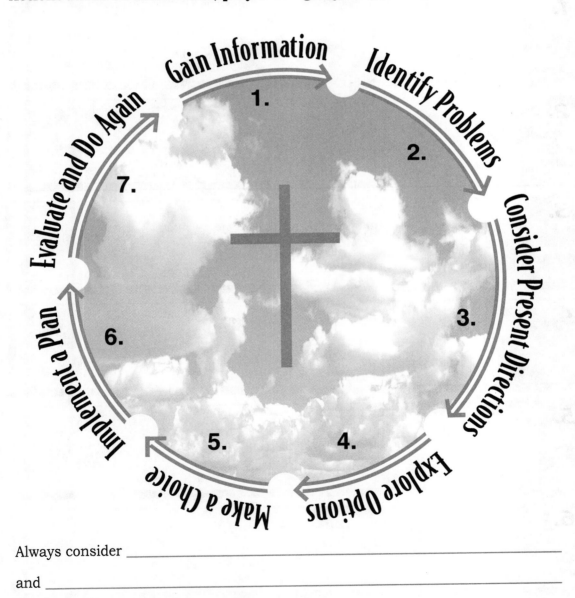

Gain Information

Identify Problems

Consider Present Directions

Explore Options

Make a Choice

Implement a Plan

Evaluate and Do Again

1.

2.

3.

4.

5.

6.

7.

Always consider _____

and _____

INQUIRY–ACTION 3.3

PRINCIPLES I'VE LEARNED ABOUT DECISION-MAKING

1.

2.

3.

4.

5.

6.

INQUIRY-ACTION 3.4

JOSHUA 24:14–15, 24

"
1 At this time, immediately	**2** for this reason ,	**3** show respect, honor	**4** determiner – a noun is next	**5** Yahweh Jehovah ,
6 obey, yield, work for	**7** objective pronoun for **5**	**8** preposition – enclosed	**9** without hypocrisy	**10** conjunction – plus
8	**11** completely honest ,•••	**10**	**12** depends on your choice	**13** pronoun for **6**
14 looks to be	**15** bad, wrong	**16** preposition – in accord with	**17** pronoun – people	**18** infinitive for verb (same as 16)
6	**4**	**5** ,	**19** decide	**20** preposition – in cause of
21 reflexive pronoun for **17**	**22** the exact one	**23** time from morning to night	**24** objective pronoun for **5**	**17**
25 future "to be" verb	**6** •••	**26** conjunction – contrast	**27** adverb – related to	**20**

43

INQUIRY-ACTION 3.4 (CONTINUED)

28 objective pronoun for self

10

29 possessive pronoun for self

30 home, family **,**

31 pronoun – all of us

25

6

4

5 **"** **.**

10

4

32 persons of Israel

33 spoke, told

16

34 writer of book **" ,**

4

5

35 possessive pronoun – belongs to us

36 Supreme Being

37 subjective pronoun for **32**

25

6 **,**

10

38 possessive pronoun for **5**

39 spoken words

37

25

40 submit and do **"** **.**

LEAH

Surviving Rejection

Feeling rejected? Do you feel that no matter how hard you try, you still mess up? Do you feel like an "outsider" in your own church or in your own school? Do you always think that things will get better tomorrow, but they never do?

If you feel like you are the only one who has ever experienced failure and rejection, read on!

✦ Beethoven's music teacher was quoted as saying, "As a composer, he is hopeless." However, Beethoven went on to become one of the most famous composers this world has ever known.

✦ Thomas Edison was a very poor student. Matter of fact, some of his teachers felt that he would never finish school. Yet Edison's inventions touch the lives of individuals around the world.

✦ F. W. Woolworth got a job in a store when he was 21 but was not allowed to wait on customers because he "did not have enough sense." Yet before his life was over, he had established a chain of stores that would change the way people shopped for the next 50 years.

✦ Louisa May Alcott was told by an editor that she would never write anything with popular appeal. Yet she became the author of several literary classics including *Little Women*.

✦ Abraham Lincoln's road to the White House was not exactly paved with success. He was a failure in business in 1831. He was defeated for the legislature in 1832. He failed at business again in 1833 and then had a nervous breakdown in 1836. In 1838 he was defeated as Speaker of the House and then lost as elector in 1840. He lost in Congress in both 1843 and 1848. He was defeated for the Senate in 1855 and then overturned for Vice-President in 1856. However, in 1860 he was elected President of the United States. To this day he is considered the most important president in our nation's history.

Can you imagine the feelings of failure and rejection these people must have felt? There are thousands of stories of individuals who have experienced the pain of rejection and gone on to fame and success. At some time or another, everyone faces rejection. How you face that rejection will determine your future success.

Leah's story (Genesis 29) illustrates the pain of rejection. She did not deserve the treatment she received at the hands of Jacob (or her father). There is no indication that she ever harmed anyone. She always respected her parents and was obedient to God. Yet she had to endure terrible rejection.

The story began as Jacob departed from Canaan escaping to his mother's brother, Laban. He was running from a hostile brother whom he had deceived and who now sought his life. Upon arriving at a shepherds' well in Haran, he saw Rachel and fell hopelessly in love with her.

The Bible tells us (Genesis 29:16) that Jacob's uncle Laban had two daughters. The older daughter's name was Leah. She is described as having an eye problem. Rachel was the younger daughter. Rachel is described as ". . . beautiful of form and appearance" (Genesis 29:17).

Jacob agreed to work for Laban for seven years to earn the right to marry Rachel. In Jacob's mind, seven years was a small price to pay for someone as beautiful as Rachel. This is obvious from the words of Genesis 29:20, ". . . they (the seven years) seemed only a few days for him because of the love he had for her."

But Laban had no intention of keeping his side of the bargain. When the wedding day arrived, Laban deceived Jacob and gave him Leah instead of Rachel for his wife. Accomplishing this plan of deception was not difficult. The ceremonial wedding veil would not allow Jacob to see his bride. The darkness of the night prevented him from knowing his bride was Leah until the next morning.

Jacob immediately went to Laban, accusing him of not fulfilling the bargain. He demanded that Rachel be given to him as his wife. Laban responded that their customs would not allow the younger daughter to be married before the older daughter. Therefore, Laban had no choice but to give him Leah first.

Now that Jacob had married Leah, Laban made him a new offer. If Jacob would serve for another seven years, he would also be given Rachel as his wife. Jacob agreed, and a week later he also married Rachel.

However, this is not a "and they lived happily ever after" story. Upon marrying Rachel, the Bible says, ". . . and he loved Rachel more than Leah . . ." (Genesis 29:30). It was clear that Jacob rejected Leah. Can you imagine what it must have been like to experience what Leah did?

Jacob, as well as Leah's family, had made beauty the basis upon which to determine the value of a person. While it is certainly not wrong to try to look our best, it is wrong to judge people based upon their appearance. The comments of Jacob and Laban demonstrate that beauty was extremely important to them. As a result, Leah was constantly compared to Rachel's beauty.

Leah was deeply hurt as a result of her rejection. This is obvious from the names she gave to her first three children. According to Genesis 29:32–34, the meanings of Reuben, Simeon and Levi point to the lack of love and acceptance by Jacob. She hoped that her sons would cause Jacob to love her. But she soon learned that Jacob still rejected her.

Yet in God's plan, Leah was not rejected. In fact, Leah is one of the most blessed women in the Old Testament. You have certainly heard of the twelve tribes of Israel. It is through Leah that six sons were born, sons who would head six of the twelve tribes. Eventually two tribes would live in the southern region of Palestine and be known as Judah, the name of her fourth son.

God blessed Leah in even a greater way. It would be through Judah that Jesus the Messiah would eventually be born. According to Luke 3:30, the family of Judah would include David, thus becoming the messianic line. Jesus fulfilled prophecy as He became the Lion of Judah.

Right now, you may feel rejected. You may even feel like no one cares and that you have no future. But God has not rejected you. He cares for you. He has set before you a future that is full of opportunities. Listen to just a few of His promises:

"I will never leave you nor forsake (reject) you" (Hebrews 13:5).

"casting all your care upon Him, for he cares for you" (1 Peter 5:7).

". . . I chose you and appointed you that you should go and bear fruit . . ." (John 15:16).

If you face rejection in your own strength, you will fail. If you face rejection in the power that only God can provide, you will be victorious. How do you plan to face rejection? In your own strength, or in God's strength? The choice is yours!

INQUIRY-ACTION 4.1

LEAH AND RACHEL

Compare and contrast Rachel to Leah as you check the references provided.

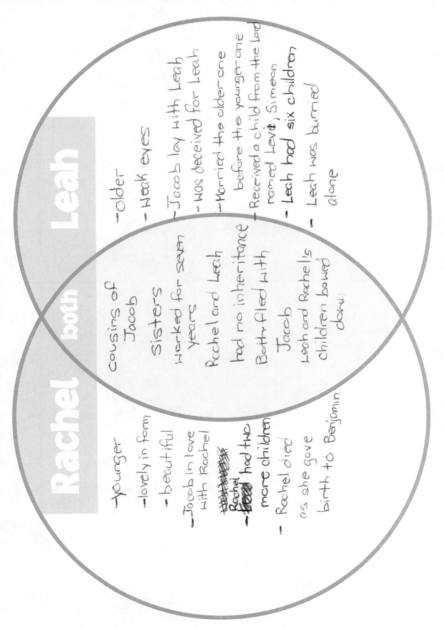

Leah
- older
- weak eyes
- Jacob lay with Leah
- was deceived for Leah
- Married the older one before the younger one
- Received a child from the lord named Levi, Simeon
- Leah had six children
- Leah was burried alone

both
- cousins of Jacob
- sisters
- worked for seven years
- Rachel and Leah had no inheritance
- Both fled with Jacob
- Leah and Rachel's children bowed down

Rachel
- younger
- lovely in form
- beautiful
- Jacob in love with Rachel
- ~~Rachel~~ ~~had the~~ had the more children
- Rachel died as she gave birth to Benjamin

INQUIRY–ACTION 4.2

SUGGESTIONS ON HOW TO HANDLE REJECTION

1. _____

_____

_____

2. _____

_____

_____

3. _____

_____

_____

4. _____

_____

_____

5. _____

_____

_____

6. _____

_____

_____

INQUIRY-ACTION 4.3

OVERCOMING REJECTION

To Overcome Rejection, I Absolutely Must:

◆ Accept that God _____

_____

_____

◆ Accept that Jesus _____

_____

_____

◆ Know that God has a future _____

_____

_____

It Helps When:

◆ I have family and friends who _____

_____

_____

_____

_____

INQUIRY-ACTION 4.3 (CONTINUED)

✦ I can talk about _____

_____

_____

_____

_____

_____

✦ I am careful not to act _____

_____

_____

_____

_____

_____

✦ I focus on activities that _____

_____

_____

_____

_____

_____

INQUIRY-ACTION 4.4

NATURAL   VS.   SUPERNATURAL

▼ **Become Bitter**

▼ **Get Revenge**

▼ **Withdraw**

▼ **Choose Wrong
Relationships**

▼ **Hurt Myself**

INQUIRY-ACTION 4.5

JOHN 6:37 AND 39

Circle the words for the passage from the Bible version selected and write them below.

allbutthatthesomefatherwillgivesgivethmecome
tomethosethefatherhasgivenmeandtheonewhoe
verhimthatcomescomethtomeIwillbynomeansce
rtainlyinnowiseneverdriveawaynevernotreject
castoutthemandthisisthefatherswillofthefather
godhimwhichhathwhosentmethatIshouldshallno
tloseevennoneoneofallthatthosewhichofallheha
thhasgivenmeIshouldlosenothingbutthatIshoul
draiseitthemuptoeternallifeagainatonthelastday

_____

_____

_____

_____

_____

_____

_____

_____

NEHEMIAH

Surviving Peer Pressure

If you're like most young people, you are looking forward to getting your driver's license. Let's suppose, for a few minutes, that you not only have your driver's license, but you have a beautiful new sports car as well. Imagine that you have pulled onto the main highway, ready to take one of the most exciting—and dangerous—trips of your life.

Your destination is "Adultsville." You will probably arrive there in about eight to ten years. You have just passed through the little town of "Puberty" and are now out in the countryside known as "Teen Land." You have encountered a few bumps in the road. However, for the most part, it has been a smooth trip. That's all about to change.

Up ahead you see warning lights and a flagman motioning you to stop. As you bring your shiny sports car to a halt, the flagman approaches your vehicle calmly, but with a very serious tone in his voice. "The canyon walls are unstable and numerous rock slides have blocked the road," he says. "If you proceed, you'll face great danger." Turning back is not an option, however. You can only go forward.

"Want some advice?" the flagman asks. "Proceed slowly. Be on the lookout for falling boulders at all times. KEEP RIGHT!! You will come to a road that takes you around the rock slide and puts you back on the main highway to Adultsville."

By now you have probably figured out what this story is all about. Of course, you are the driver of the sports car. The sports car represents your life as you travel the road from childhood to adulthood. The flagman could be your parents, pastor or teacher. The rock slide is peer pressure.

Everyone traveling the highway from childhood to adulthood encounters the dangers of peer pressure. Although the warning signs are clear, many young people ignore them. They find themselves overwhelmed by the pelting stones and plunge over the edge. Their journey to "Adultsville" is interrupted. For some young people the fall is so great that they are never able to complete their trip.

The advice of the flagman is clear: "KEEP RIGHT!" If you have a difficult time remembering the flagman's advice, just pay close attention the next time you are traveling down the highway around your home. You will not go far before you see a sign that says "Keep Right." Every time you see that sign, imagine that it is God's reminder to you to avoid the rock slide of peer pressure.

Everyone faces some type of peer pressure. Peer pressure is not unique to this period of history, nor is it reserved only for teenagers. It is a normal part of life but has a particularly strong influence over an individual during adolescence.

Why are individuals influenced by what other people think and say? The simple answer is: Most people don't like to "stand out" or be different from those around them. This fact is clearly understood by the advertising industry. If advertisers can convince enough people that a certain fashion style is "in" or a particular automobile is the most popular, they know that others will purchase the same products. Psychologists have called this phenomenon the "bandwagon" effect or "herd mentality." Those are just fancy names for how people respond to peer pressure.

Although peer pressure affects all ages, its influence is most strongly felt during adolescence. Why is this so? Unfortunately, this question is not so easy to answer.

The primary reason that adolescents respond to peer pressure is the same as children and adults. There is the desire to "be like" those around them. In this time of life you naturally transition from dependence on parents into responsible self-direction. During this process you will face some awkward times of uncertainty which make you over-sensitive and dependent on the thoughts and feelings of others. As you grow in establishing personal values and decision-making, this sensitivity to peer pressure will decrease.

During adolescence the desire to "fit in" is more intense and plays a greater role in the teenager's decisions and actions. This occurs for any of the following reasons:

- The belief that "No one will like me" if I don't dress, talk or act like everyone else.
- The belief that in order to be considered mature I have to "prove" my independence by making my own decisions.
- The belief that my "security" comes as a result of the friends that I have.
- The belief that the values and principles that I have been taught in the past are now "old fashioned" and "stupid."

As you can see, young people respond to peer pressure for many different reasons. In many cases, the peer pressure poses no threat. However, the desire to conform sometimes becomes dangerous when you are pushed to do things that you know are wrong. That is why the Apostle Paul, in Romans 12:2, warns us "DO NOT BE CONFORMED!" The desire to be like others can be so strong that . . .

- you can be tempted to reject what your parents have taught you.
- you deny that God has any authority in your life.
- you reject values you have always believed in.
- you are willing to do things which may seriously harm you.

Maybe you have never thought about this before, but peer pressure is not always negative. There are many examples in history of great men and women who have used peer pressure in a positive way to accomplish great tasks. Nehemiah is one example.

When Nehemiah determined to rebuild the walls of Jerusalem and restore worship in the Temple, there was plenty of negative peer pressure already in the city. Because they were bowing down to false gods, the inhabitants of the city didn't welcome Nehemiah's attempts to restore worship. Many of the Jewish leaders were unhappy with Nehemiah's arrival because they had married foreign wives, a clear violation of God's Laws. And finally, Nehemiah faced opposition from Israel's enemies. Sanballat (a Samaritan), Tobiah (an Amorite) and Geshem (an Arab) controlled much of the city's wealth. They certainly did all they could to prevent Nehemiah's success.

Nehemiah faced a very difficult task for a number of reasons. First, rebuilding the city's walls was going to require great time, effort and cooperation. Second, there were enemies living in Jerusalem who were only interested in profit. Nehemiah knew they would take every possible step to stop his work. The most difficult challenge he faced, however, was providing leadership to the Jews. They pressured him to give up the idea of rebuilding the walls. They refused to help him. They even told him to leave Jerusalem and return home. Now, that's peer pressure!

But Nehemiah did not let the negative influences stop him. He reminded the people that God had led him to complete this task (Nehemiah 6:3). He then stood up to those who were ridiculing him and acknowledged God as the true God of Israel (Nehemiah 4:5, 13). His response clearly demonstrated that he was committed to doing what was right (Nehemiah 5:14–18). Nehemiah depended on God's help, available through prayer (Nehemiah 1:6; 4:4–5; 6:9).

As a result of his firm stand, others rallied to help him. No longer was he standing alone. An increasing number of Jews joined with him to stand against those who opposed God. They assisted in the task God had given to Nehemiah to complete. Nehemiah was determined to KEEP RIGHT! regardless of the pressure to conform to the desires of his peers.

No matter what age you are, you are influenced by peer pressure. Through Nehemiah's life and leadership, you can see that God blesses those who KEEP RIGHT!, even when everyone is against you.

As you travel your personal road to "Adultsville," pay close attention to the peer pressure in front of you. Each time you are tempted to conform to the pressures of the group, ask yourself the following questions:

- ✦ Will my decision/action dishonor God?
- ✦ Will my decision/action upset my parents?
- ✦ Will my decision/action harm me or others?

The decision to KEEP RIGHT! is yours to make.

INQUIRY-ACTION 5.1

NEHEMIAH IDENTIFIES A NEED

I. What is the historical context for Nehemiah?

A. _____

_____

B. _____

_____

C. _____

_____

II. Who was Nehemiah?

A. _____

_____

B. _____

_____

C. _____

_____

D. _____

_____

INQUIRY–ACTION 5.1 (CONTINUED)

NEHEMIAH IDENTIFIES A NEED

III. **What were the obstacles Nehemiah faced?**

A. _____

B. _____

C. _____

D. _____

E. _____

F. _____

G. _____

_____   _____

_____   _____

_____   _____

IV. **What tactics did these enemies use to pressure Nehemiah to give up?**

A. _____

B. _____

C. _____

D. _____

INQUIRY-ACTION 5.2

1. Why are teenagers easily influenced by peer pressure?

Because they have this wild desire to fit in with their friends and everybody else.

2. Why can peer pressure be dangerous?

Because it clouds your judgments on things like moral values, independence, and your relationship w/ God.

3. What does "giving in" to peer pressure say about the individual?

It say's that the individual is weak in temptation and would rather allow others to think for him rather than theirselves.

4. What is the best advice, thus far, on how to respond to negative peer pressure?

Ignore it, Ask God for help, ask yourself will it ruin your family, friendship, relationship w/ God.

INQUIRY-ACTION 5.3

"JUST THE FACTS"

There is a lot of misunderstanding about what peer pressure really is. Your teacher will give you "just the facts" about peer pressure. Record them in the space provided below, and use this handy "fact" sheet when you are faced with peer pressure.

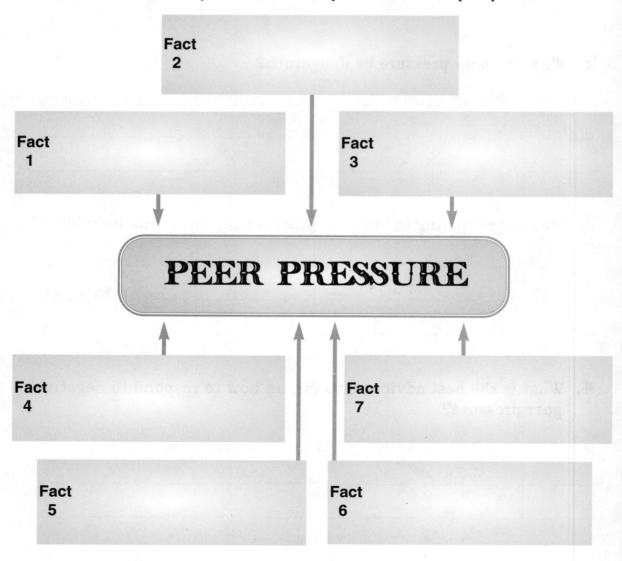

Fact 2

Fact 1

Fact 3

PEER PRESSURE

Fact 4

Fact 7

Fact 5

Fact 6

INQUIRY-ACTION 5.4

PROVERBS 4:14–15, 18–19

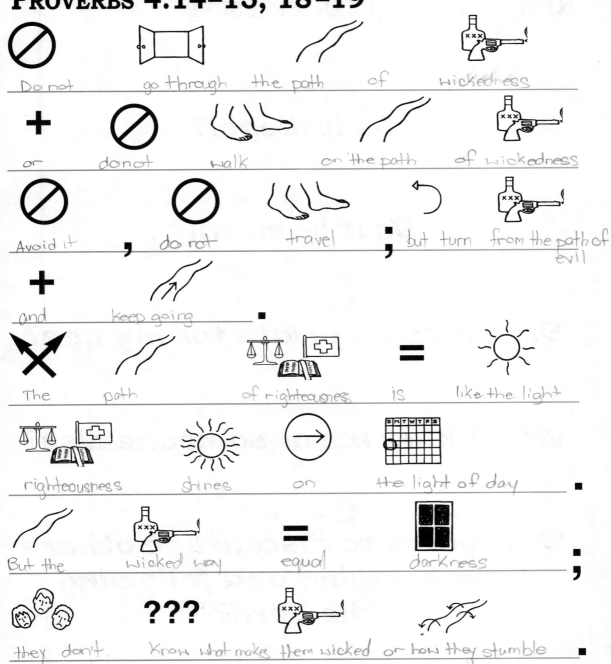

Do not   go through   the path   of   wickedness

or   do not   walk   on the path   of wickedness

Avoid it   ,   do not   travel   ; but turn   from the path of evil

and   keep going .

The   path   of righteousness   is   like the light

righteousness   shines   on   the light of day .

But the   wicked way   equal   darkness ;

they don't.   **???** Know what makes them wicked   or how they stumble on it. .

INQUIRY-ACTION 5.4 (CONTINUED)

RESPONDING TO PEER PRESSURE

Question 1:
Is it illegal?

Question 2:
Is it immoral?

Question 3:
Is it inappropriate for my age?

Question 4:
Will it hurt me or someone else?

Question 5:
Is it going to discourage others from knowing and following the Lord?

MARY (MOTHER OF JESUS)

Surviving Family Stress

The "Big Day" for Romeo had finally arrived! He was going on a journey that he was sure no Jack Russell terrier had ever taken before. It would be the trip of a lifetime. He would see every sight and smell every smell for the nearly 3,000 miles from Tucson, Arizona, to Lexington, Kentucky. It was Christmas and he was on his way to "Grandma's house."

The ride in the car was not as much fun as he had thought. Even though he got to sit in the front seat with his parents (the human ones, that is) everything went by so fast that it made him dizzy. He was always glad when they stopped and he could get out, run and snoop out the surroundings.

Of course, he also had to have his leash on. He knew that Jack Russell terriers had a reputation for wanting to run free and follow their noses. Matter of fact, he had even heard that some of his friends, who had gotten loose, ran so far that they became lost. That was a scary thought.

Although he would never think of leaving his "parents" and his home, the thought of running and running and running—with no leash anywhere in sight—was so exciting! If only he had the chance.

As the hours passed, Romeo dreamed of what Lexington would be like. He had been told that there were lots of farms, beautiful fences, probably some snow (something they didn't have in Tucson) and horses! He had been told that they were HUGE animals and that he had better stay out of their way. He couldn't wait to get there!

The moment finally arrived. There was Grandma's house (at least that's what he was told) straight ahead. He couldn't help but notice that it was a big house, it was made of bricks, and—he couldn't believe his eyes—it had no fence! The house was so new that the landscaping and fence had not been completed. He would be able to see everything going on in the neighborhood.

"This is a neat house," he thought as he ran from room to room. There were stairs to play on, windows to look out and, of course, there was Rhett. Rhett was just like the Scottish terriers that he had seen in picture books. He wondered if Rhett was going to be his friend while he was visiting. But that's another story. He was at Grandma's for Christmas and life couldn't be better.

Was it the excitement of getting there or the activity of bringing all the luggage and presents into the house? Whatever it was, no one noticed that the front door had been left open—wide open! This was his chance to explore the neighborhood, run in the snow and maybe even see a horse.

As Romeo scooted out the door, his parents caught a glimpse of what had happened. Frantically, they grabbed their coats and pursued him. One chased him on foot while the other hopped into the car to corner him at the end of the street.

For the next 30 minutes it was a game of "catch-me-if-you-can." Romeo had never had so much fun in his entire life. It's too bad that his parents didn't seem to be enjoying it. In fact, they had this worried, scared look on their faces.

Finally, the "chase" was over. Romeo was cornered in a neighbor's garage when he went in to check it out. He was now in his parents' arms as they carried him back to their car. They seemed so tired and stressed. Had he really upset them that much?

Can you identify with the family stress experienced by Romeo's parents? Although we love our pets and they bring great joy to our lives, they can also be a source of great stress at times.

But stress caused by taking care of a pet is minor compared to the many other stresses facing families today. Although there are times that you may feel you are the only one facing pressures at home, stress is not unique to your family. Stress is a fact of life and exists in every family.

Although Christmas is still a few weeks away, think for a moment about the "Christmas story" recorded in Luke 2:1–20. The story of Mary, Joseph and the birth of Jesus is probably one of the most familiar stories in all of the world. Have you ever thought about the family stress experienced by Mary and Joseph during this time? Think about how any of the following events would cause stress in their lives:

- the angel's announcement to Mary (Luke 1:28)
- the realization that her child would be the Messiah (Luke 1:31–33)
- the fact that she was not yet married (Luke 1:34)
- Joseph's thoughts on whether to divorce Mary (Matthew 1:19)
- the difficult trip to Bethlehem (Luke 2:1–4)
- giving birth alone in a manger (Luke 2:7)
- the visits of strangers (Luke 2:8–19)
- Joseph warned of Herod's plan (Matthew 2:13)
- the escape to Egypt (Matthew 2:14–15)
- male children killed (Matthew 2:16–18)
- living away from family and friends (Matthew 2:21–23)

In addition to these stressful events, Mary and Joseph experienced another type of stress as well. Certainly, Mary's pregnancy caused a lot of "talk" in town. Some would wonder who the father was. Others would speak of the shame she had brought to herself and her family. Mary, Joseph and their families must have been hurt by the gossip going around.

But with God's help, Mary was able to rise above the pressures of family stress. Her ability to overcome these difficult times was made possible because she understood two important principles.

First, she knew that God was in total control. Everything that was taking place in her life was being orchestrated by God. No matter what happened or what people said, it was not a surprise to God. As a result, she could withstand the stress she experienced.

Second, she humbly accepted what God had brought into her life. In Luke 1:38 she said to the angel of the Lord, "Let it be to me according to Your word." Although she did not understand all that was to take place in her life, she accepted God's plan and moved forward in faith.

Are you experiencing family stress today? It may be that your parents are not getting along or don't even live with each other any more. Criticism and anger may be common in the ways that your family members talk to each other. Your home may face the consequences of alcohol or drug abuse.

No matter how difficult the stress may be, you can rise above it if you will follow Mary's example. First of all, remember that God is in control of your life. He understands the heartache you feel. Second, accept your circumstances as part of God's plan for your life. Remember, God uses the events of our lives to mold and shape us for future service to Him. The difficult times that you are now experiencing may be part of God's "advanced training" for a special task He has for you in the future.

When faced with family stress, the psalmist wrote the following:

> "I will say of the Lord, He is my refuge
> and my fortress: my God; in Him I will trust."
> (Psalm 91:2)

Your response to family stress should be:

✦ Realize that God is in complete control.
✦ Accept the circumstances as part of His plan for your life.
✦ Trust Him to protect and guide you at all times.

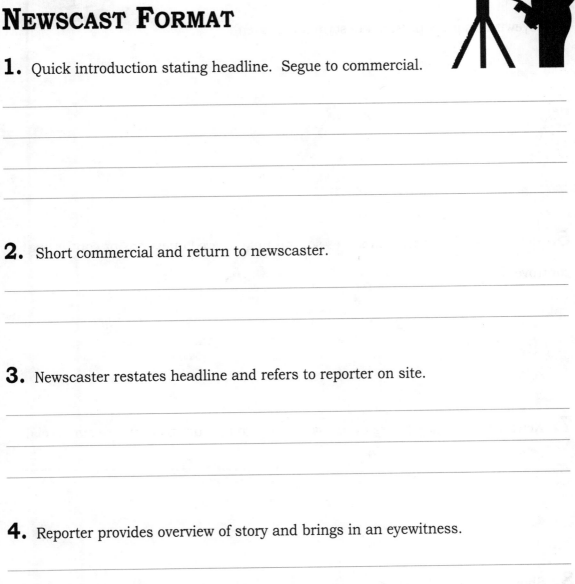

INQUIRY-ACTION 6.1

NEWSCAST FORMAT

1. Quick introduction stating headline. Segue to commercial.

2. Short commercial and return to newscaster.

3. Newscaster restates headline and refers to reporter on site.

4. Reporter provides overview of story and brings in an eyewitness.

INQUIRY–ACTION 6.1 (CONTINUED)

5. Eyewitness gives personal description of events.

_____

_____

_____

_____

6. Reporter summarizes and states several unanswered questions or continuing controversies.

_____

_____

_____

7. Newscaster quickly states overview of story and segues to another commercial.

_____

_____

_____

8. Short commercial.

_____

_____

INQUIRY-ACTION 6.2

List two areas in which you can identify with the family pressures faced by Mary. Explain the situations. Then write about your part in adding to the stress or making the problem worse.

INQUIRY–ACTION 6.3

SUGGESTIONS FOR MANAGING FAMILY STRESS

INQUIRY-ACTION 6.3 (CONTINUED)

INQUIRY-ACTION 6.4

COLOSSIANS 3:18–21

Who: **Wives**, _____
_____

Command: _____
_____

Whom: _____
_____

Reason _____
_____

Whom: _____
_____

Who: **Husbands**, _____
_____

Command: _____
_____

Whom: _____
_____

Command: _____
_____

Whom: _____
_____

Who: **Children**, _____
_____

Command: _____
_____

Whom: _____
_____

How: _____
_____

Reason _____
_____

Whom: _____
_____

Who: **Fathers**, _____
_____

Command: _____
_____

Whom: _____
_____

Reason _____
_____

TIMOTHY

Surviving Lack of Confidence

YOU ARE NOT A NOBODY! Although your English teacher wouldn't like the construction of the sentence, it does effectively convey the message. Put aside your feelings of worthlessness and inadequacy. If your desire is to increase in confidence, then you must begin by realizing that YOU ARE NOT A NOBODY! In fact, YOU ARE SOMEBODY SPECIAL!

• Dwight L. Moody was one of America's greatest evangelists. But his fame does not end there. At a time when the Young Men's Christian Association (YMCA) was struggling to survive, he was made its president. Under his leadership the association became strong and prospered. Before his ministry ended, Mr. Moody had started the first Bible school of its kind in the country, the Chicago Evangelization Society (later called Moody Bible Institute).

When Dwight L. Moody was a young man, he worked as a shoe salesman in Chicago. One day a Sunday School teacher came to buy a pair of shoes, and he took the opportunity to talk to Mr. Moody about his need of a Savior. It was at that point that Dwight L. Moody accepted the Lord as his Savior.

> **Question:** *What was the name of the Sunday School teacher who led Dwight L. Moody to the Lord?*

• William Carey has been called the "father of modern missions." He saw how difficult it was for missionaries to gain the necessary support and the resources they needed. As a result, he helped to organize the English Baptist Missionary Society. This society became the model for many other mission groups. As the number of groups increased, so did the number of missionaries.

In addition to the formation of the English Baptist Missionary Society, Mr. Carey became one of its first missionaries to India. Today his ministry is still considered one of the most important works in all the world.

Question: *What person financed Mr. Carey's first trip to India?*

• The greatest discovery of ancient manuscripts in recent times, the Dead Sea Scrolls, were found near the Dead Sea in 1947. The Scrolls contained ancient texts of parts of the Old Testament, as well as writings that originated between the Old and New Testament periods. The Dead Sea Scrolls make up the oldest existing manuscripts of the Bible in any language.

The Dead Sea Scrolls were not discovered by archaeologists working in the area around the Dead Sea. They were found by a shepherd boy playing in a cave south of Jericho.

Question: *What was the name of that shepherd boy?*

• Elijah, the great prophet of God, is found feeling sorry for himself in 1 Kings 19. It seems that Jezebel is trying to kill him. Elijah finally cries out to God ". . . I alone am left" (verse 14). As far as Elijah was concerned, he was the only one left in the whole world who was remaining faithful to God.

But God informed Elijah that he was wrong. According to verse 18, there were still 7,000 men in Israel who had not bowed down to worship Baal.

Question: *Can you name just one of those 7,000 faithful individuals?*

• In the last chapter of the book of Romans, Paul is giving his greetings to those who had been especially important to him in his ministry. Some of the names include Epaenetus, Andronicus, Junia, Amplia, Urbance, Stachys and Apelles. As a matter of fact, there are 16 more names on this list, names that never appear on any other page in history.

Question: *Do you have any idea what any of these people did?*

By now you should be getting the picture. Had it not been for these "nobodies," the entire course of history could be different. Although unknown to us, these men and women were a significant part of God's plan. They moved forward in complete confidence, knowing He was guiding their lives.

Today there are many who lack confidence and are unsure of themselves. This is because their confidence is misplaced. Some place their confidence in people, believing that others will make up for their lack of ability. Some place their confidence in position, thinking that if they could just "make the team" or "get elected," everything would be all right. And others place their confidence in possessions, trusting money and things to give them the security they desire.

Confidence does not come from knowing the right people, attaining a certain position or having a lot of possessions. Your personal relationship to God and your understanding of what He has done for you determine the strength of your confidence. This important fact is summarized in the following "Confidence Principles."

Principle 1: God's Creation

You are God's unique creation. That means that there is no one else in all the world just like you! Because God has created you, you can be confident that He loves you and desires only the best for you.

Principle 2: God's Opinion

You care about what other people think of you. That's only natural. But it is God's opinion of you that really counts in this life—and for all eternity. He is the One who will never leave you or forsake you (Deuteronomy 31:6). You can have confidence, knowing that He will stand by you, no matter what happens.

Principle 3: God's Plan

Although it may not seem like it at times, God has a specific plan for your life. You can go through life confidently each day knowing that the God of this universe is in complete control. He is not taken by surprise. He is working out His eternal plan through you.

These "Confidence Principles" clearly made a difference in Timothy's life. Timothy had been given great responsibility over the church of Ephesus by the Apostle Paul. This was an established church that needed a strong leader. However, Timothy also knew that he was going to face some very difficult challenges in his ministry. Paul had warned him of the false teachers, liars, blasphemers and persecution that he would face. In addition to all of this, Timothy was young and inexperienced.

If there was ever an individual who lacked confidence, it was Timothy! Paul wrote to him to be strong and have courage as he rebuked, corrected, preached and instructed the Ephesus church. Timothy overcame his natural tendency toward shyness and timidity, but not by trusting in himself. He knew that he was uniquely created by God, that God loved him and that the responsibilities he now had were a part of God's plan for his life.

In what areas of your life do you lack confidence today? Are you concerned about what you are going to face when you enter high school? Does meeting new people make you nervous? Are you unsure about some personal decisions that you are facing?

It is God's desire that Christians experience confidence in their lives. He does not want you to live in fear or to dread the future. He wants you to remember that YOU ARE NOT A NOBODY—GOING NOWHERE! You are a child of the King. You are loved by Him. He has a special plan for you life. Be confident!!

"For God has not given us the spirit of fear
but of power, love and a sound mind."
(2 Timothy 1:7)

INQUIRY-ACTION 7.1

Dear Tim,

INQUIRY-ACTION 7.1 (CONTINUED)

INQUIRY-ACTION 7.2

STUDY GUIDE — TIMOTHY

❶ How did Timothy learn about the Lord? (2 Timothy 1:4–5; 3:14–15; Acts 16:1–2)

_____

_____

_____

❷ What do we know about Timothy's father? (Acts 16:1)

_____

_____

_____

❸ What relationship developed between Paul and Timothy? (1 Timothy 1:2a, 18a; Acts 16:1–3a; 2 Timothy 1:2, 4; Romans 16:21; 1 Corinthians 4:17; Philemon 1:1)

_____

_____

_____

_____

❹ What kinds of people challenged Timothy in the Ephesus church?
(Acts 20:20–30; 1 Timothy 4:1; 1 Timothy 1:3–7, 19–20; 4:1–2; 5:13; 6:3–5, 20b–21; 2 Timothy 2:16–18; 3:1–5)

_____

_____

_____

INQUIRY-ACTION 7.2 (CONTINUED)

❺ What was Timothy told to do? (List only verb command words.) (1 Timothy 1:3; 4:6, 11; 6:12, 18, 21; 2 Timothy 1:6, 8; 2:1, 3, 14, 24; 3:14; 4:2, 5)

_____

_____

_____

❻ Why might these commands be difficult for Timothy?

_____

_____

_____

❼ What was Paul's instruction and encouragement? (1 Timothy 1:18–19a; 2:8; 4:7, 11–16; 6:11–12; 2 Timothy 1:6, 8, 13; 2:3, 22; 3:14; 4:2)

_____

_____

_____

❽ Does it seem that Timothy listened to Paul's instruction? (Revelation 2:1–3)

_____

_____

_____

❾ What lessons have you learned about timid people living for God?

_____

_____

_____

INQUIRY-ACTION 7.3

God's Part		My Part
God	• • •	*I will*
Isaiah 41:13; Psalm 46:1–3; Ephesians 1:19–20	(therefore)	Psalm 66:8–9; Psalm 56:10–11; Joel 2:21
God	• • •	*I will*
1 Peter 5:7; Psalm 112:7–8; Hebrews 13:5–6		Psalm 56:3; Psalm 118:8–9; Isaiah 41:13
God	• • •	*I will*
Psalm 34:4; 1 John 5:14; Isaiah 58:9		Philippians 4:6; Hebrews 4:16; Psalm 18:6, 18–19
God	• • •	*I will*
Isaiah 41:10; John 14:27; Psalm 73:23–26		Psalm 18:32; Philippians 4:13; 1 Chronicles 28:20

INQUIRY-ACTION 7.4

2 TIMOTHY 1:7 AND 1 TIMOTHY 4:12

Use the words in the bank to write the verses.

a	look
an	love
and	mind
are	no
anyone	not
be	of
because	on
believers	one
but	power
conduct	purity
despise	self-
did	discipline
don't	set
down	sound
example	speech
faith	spirit
fear	the
for	timidity
give	to
given	us
God	ward
has	you
in	your
let	young
life	youth

ABRAHAM

Surviving an Unknown Future

You only get three guesses. Are you ready? Who was awarded the prestigious "Woman of the World" award just a couple of years before her death?

Need a hint? This lady was also named "Most Admired Woman" for three consecutive years. Who is she?

If you guessed Mother Teresa, winner of the Nobel Peace Prize, you're wrong. Former First Lady Barbara Bush? You're wrong again. Maybe you guessed the former Prime Minister of Great Britain, Mrs. Margaret Thatcher. You are wrong for the third time. None of these ladies received the honor of being named both "Woman of the World" and "Most Admired Woman."

Who was this "mystery lady"? None other than the world's most famous astrologer, Jeanne Dixon. Over the course of her lifetime she achieved the status of royalty and power because others believed that she could foretell the future. Some of the wealthiest and most powerful people in the world came to her for advice. As she would begin to predict their future, she would confidently say, "Behold the revelation of your destiny."

Fortune telling, looking into a crystal ball and other gimmicks for predicting the future were once associated with witchcraft. These practices were considered evil, part hoax and part superstition, all practiced in a cloak of secrecy and darkness. These activities are no longer done behind closed doors. Predicting the future has become big business. From television's "Psychic Hot-Line" to the many books and games available in the mall, "knowing the future" has become an obsession in today's society.

The increasing interest in predicting the future demonstrates the growing fear and uncertainty of what the future will bring. As a result, many people seek answers from a "mystical world." If you're curious about these areas, substitute the word "demonic" for "mystical." Satan is the ruler of the underworld, and all such activities are demonic. Remember, the Bible clearly forbids us to be involved in magic, sorcery and divination (Deuteronomy 18:10–11).

God never intended for us to gaze into a crystal ball or purchase a computer program to discern the future. He directed James to write:

> Come now, you who say, "Today or tomorrow, we will go to such and such a city, spend a year there, buy and sell and make a profit"; whereas you do not know what will happen tomorrow. For what is your life? It is even a vapor that appears for a little time and then vanishes away. Instead you ought to say, "If the Lord wills, we shall live and do this or that."
>
> (James 4:13–15)

Throughout the Bible, God's lessons regarding the future are clear: Walk by faith with God now and leave the future completely in His hands. From our human perspective, the future is unknown. But God is never taken by surprise.

It took Abraham many years to learn to walk with God by faith. Yet the lessons learned by Abraham are so important that 39 of the 50 chapters in the book of Genesis are devoted to him and his children. God gives more detail about Abraham than He does about Creation.

Abraham was born and raised in Ur of the Chaldees, a seaport city on the Persian Gulf. Ur was a focal point for trading and commerce in the entire region. It was a large city, inhabited by people from all over the eastern world.

If you could see pictures of Ur, you would quickly notice at least two conspicuous buildings in the city. These were known as ziggurats, or temple towers. They were places of worship patterned after the Tower of Babel. These towers were square, terraced and built of brick. One was dedicated to Nannar, the moon-god, and the other to Ningal, his wife. Life in Ur was centered around business and pagan worship.

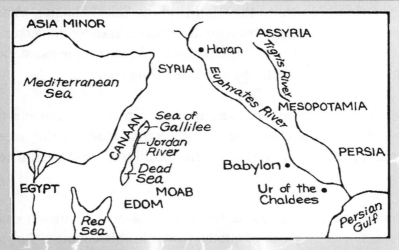

These were just two of the reasons that God spoke to Abraham and said, "Get out of your country, and from your family, and from your father's house, to a land that I will show you" (Genesis 12:1). All of God's history (His story) features two groups of people: the nation Israel and the Church. The nation of Israel was the family through which Jesus would come. Abraham was to be the father of this nation. However, God wanted Abraham removed from false gods.

As Abraham prepared to leave his homeland, he faced an unknown future. He must have asked himself at least the following questions:

What is this promised land like?
How will I know when I've reached it?
Will I make it there safely? What dangers will I face?
My wife and I are old. How can I be the father of a great nation?
Will I ever return to Ur to visit my family?
What will people say—just a crazy old man?

Abraham was 75 years old when he began the 400-mile journey to Canaan. This could be considered the first step of his "walk by faith." For the next 100 years (until he died at the age of 175), he took many more steps in his walk by faith with God. These steps included trusting God to give him victory over his enemies and trusting God with the life of his son, Isaac. Each step of his faith walk gave him greater faith to take the next step.

Hebrews 11 has often been called the "Heroes of the Faith" chapter. A distinguished list of God's servants, including Abraham, is honored in these 40 verses. Yet the most noteworthy characteristic of this chapter is not the people listed, but the phrase "By faith" which is mentioned 15 times in the chapter.

Each of these men and women faced an unknown future, one step at a time, "By faith." Their faith was strong because they knew that whatever they faced, God would protect and guide them. Although they could not know the future, they knew that God did.

How much thought have you given to the future? Before you answer that question, refer to the James 4:13–15 passage quoted earlier in this chapter. Do you see the lessons about the future that God is trying to teach each of us?

His first warning to us is, **Don't count on tomorrow**. Tomorrow may not happen as you've planned. Though it isn't wrong to have a plan for the future, it is wrong to have a plan that doesn't consider God's will. Planning your life without accepting God's will is nothing more than boasting and bragging. God warns us against excluding Him from our plans.

Second, He says, **Don't dread tomorrow**. In other words, DON'T WORRY! Too many people face the unknown future in fear. This is also a sin. Our Heavenly Father knows the future and knows our needs. His grace is sufficient for anything and everything we will face.

Finally, He says, **Don't ignore tomorrow**. Although we don't know what will happen throughout the rest of our lives, we do know that one day we will spend eternity with God. Remember, the first step of the future is taken today! If you are ignoring God today, your future is uncertain. Be sure that your relationship with the Lord is right, and you won't have to worry about tomorrow.

So, what are your questions or fears as you think about the future? The lesson from Abraham, and the other heroes of the faith in Hebrews 11, is "By faith . . . ." You never need to be anxious about the future when you take each step, each day — "By faith."

INQUIRY-ACTION 8.1

SO, WHAT ABOUT THE FUTURE?

	Yes	No	Don't Know
1. I will get to where I want to go in life.			
2. I will get married.			
3. I will have children.			
4. I think making money will bring happiness.			
5. Getting a good education will be important to me.			
6. I believe God will be important in my life.			

7. I think my future career will be in _____.

8. I think the main problems of society will be _____
_____.

9. A character trait important for my future is _____
_____.

10. Regardless of my occupation, I want to do work that _____
_____.

INQUIRY-ACTION 8.2

ABRAHAM — THE MAN WHO FACED AN UNKNOWN FUTURE

_____

_____

_____

_____

_____

_____

_____

_____

_____

_____

_____

_____

_____

_____

_____

An important lesson to be learned from Abraham's life is

_____

_____

_____

_____

INQUIRY-ACTION 8.3

ABRAHAM'S UNKNOWN FUTURE

❶ Genesis 12:1

❷ Genesis 12:2

❸ Genesis 12:7

❹ Genesis 12:16

❺ Genesis 15:5

❻ Genesis 22:2

INQUIRY-ACTION 8.4

JAMES 4:13–15

1. Don't count on tomorrow.
This means I _____

_____

_____

_____

2. Don't dread tomorrow.
This means I _____

_____

_____

_____

3. Don't ignore tomorrow.
This means I _____

_____

_____

_____

INQUIRY-ACTION 8.5

HEBREWS 11:8, 10 AND 16

Use straight lines to connect all the words of the verses without going over unneeded words.

desire	knowing	heavenly	place
they	that	better	them
now	city	prepared	faith
but	a	has	Abraham
called	going	which	obeyed
their	was	waited	country
where	he	for	whose
inheritance	and	the	foundations
an	God	by	
as	out	therefore	
receive	to	go	
would	be	went	
		when	
		builder	
		maker	
		is	
		not	
		ashamed	

ABSALOM

Surviving Loss of Self-Control

The Holocaust was certainly one of the lowest periods in the history of planet Earth. During those few short years, millions of Jews were exterminated. There have been few events in the history of mankind that have approached this level of human cruelty.

Dr. Victor Frankl is one of the many courageous Jews who became a prisoner during the Holocaust. For years he endured the humiliation of the concentration camps. Fortunately, he was liberated before the Nazi exterminators had the opportunity to put him in the gas chamber.

At the beginning of his imprisonment, he was marched into a Gestapo courtroom. By the time he appeared before his accusers, everything he owned had already been taken from him. Soldiers had shaved his head and stripped all clothing off his body. He stood naked before the German high command. Forced to endure false accusations, he felt helpless and alone.

Suddenly Dr. Frankl realized there was one thing no one could ever take from him—just one. He still had the power to control his own attitude. No matter what happened to him, his choice of attitude was his to make. He could forgive or be bitter. He could cry or rejoice. He could give up or go on. He could feel sorry for himself or proclaim, "I will survive!" No one, not even the Nazi forces, could control his attitude.

Controlling your own attitude is the starting point for maintaining or regaining self-control. Remember, life is 10 percent what happens to us and 90 percent how we respond to it. The single most significant decision that you can make on a daily basis is your choice of attitude.

Absalom's lack of self-control began with an attitude problem. Absalom had good reason to be angry with his brother Amnon, who had sinned against his half-sister Tamar. But Absalom did not properly control his anger. When King David, their father, refused to punish Amnon, Absalom became further enraged. Finally, Absalom took matters into his own hands and killed Amnon. Absalom's anger had now become uncontrolled vengeance.

His lack of self-control forced him to seek safety in another country. Years later he would return to his home, only to lose control of himself once again.

Absalom was a handsome man with a great personality. Everyone seemed to like him. But his vanity got the best of him. He used his good looks and power of persuasion to have himself elected king (2 Samuel 15:7–12). He then convinced his followers to join his revolt against King David.

By the use of carefully selected spies, David learned of Absalom's attack plans and laid a trap for him in the forest at Ephraim (2 Samuel 18:1–18). Absalom's army was no match for David's experienced and well-trained troops. David's surprise attack brought immediate defeat to the rebellion, causing Absalom to flee for his life.

As Absalom fled, his mule ran beneath a spreading oak tree. Absalom's head, with its flowing thick hair, became wedged between the branches. Joab, commander of David's army, arrived and put three spears through Absalom's chest. The revolt was brought to a rapid conclusion. Absalom's lack of self-control ultimately cost him his life.

His problems with self-control began with his inability to control his attitude. He made a mental choice to focus on himself. As a result, he became spoiled, vengeful, impatient, deceitful, overly ambitious and vain. He was so despised for his actions that a large pile of stones was placed over his dead body as a sign of contempt (2 Samuel 18:17).

It is important that Christians understand the importance of their attitudes. In Philippians 2:1–2 (NASB), the Apostle Paul tells us to take charge of our own minds:

"Therefore if there is any consolation in Christ, if any comfort of love, if any fellowship of the Spirit, if any affection and mercy, fulfill my joy by being likeminded, having the same love, being of one accord, of one mind."

Paul knew that if an individual's attitudes were not under control, it would be impossible to keep actions under control. In the book of Philippians, Paul talks about three attitudes that must be true in every believer's life.

The first is an attitude of *unselfish humility.* In Philippians 2:3 (NASB) he says, "Let nothing be done through selfish ambition or conceit, but in lowliness of mind let each esteem others better than himself."

This attitude of unselfish humility was the same attitude Christ Jesus had when He came to earth to die for our sins (Philippians 2:5–8). In humility, He set aside the glory of Heaven to endure the pain of the Cross.

"Do all things without complaining and disputing" (Philippians 2:14 NASB). The second attitude we all need to possess is that of *positive encouragement.* Is complaining common in your life or at your school? Do you look for ways to encourage others, or ways to tear them down? A positive, encouraging attitude is essential to self-control.

Paul concludes by challenging us to have an attitude of *joy.* "Finally, my brethren, rejoice in the Lord" (Philippians 3:1 NASB). As we face the problems of life, joy is the oil that reduces the friction. Things occur every day that can cause us to lose self-control. Maybe someone is lying about you. Your best friend may be moving to a new city. You face struggles at home.

Immediately you have a choice to make—an attitude choice. Will you be bitter, or better? You can hand your problem to the Lord and let Him take control, or you can choose to fight and struggle on your own. An attitude of joy causes us to rejoice in every situation. Based upon the promises of God (Philippians 4:4–7), the panic we feel will be replaced by peace and strength.

When you determine to have attitudes of unselfish humility, positive encouragement and joy, you are ready to take the following steps to regain self-control.

✦ **Step One: Recognize weakness.**
Are you willing to admit that there is an area of your life that is out of control? What is it?

✦ **Step Two: Desire a change.**
Now that you have admitted the out-of-control area of your life, do you want to make a change? Are you tired of being out of control?

✦ **Step Three: Identify a strategy.**
You can't win a war without planning your battle strategy. How will you gain victory over this out-of-control behavior? What actions must you take to ensure success?

✦ **Step Four: Accept the price.**
Doing what's right is not always easy. Are you willing to pay the price, regardless of the consequences, to regain control in your life?

✦ **Step Five: God's Spirit empowers.**
Are you aware that you don't have to try to regain control in your own strength? If you will submit this out-of-control area to the Lord, He will give you the strength to regain control.

✦ **Step Six: Take action. Do what's right.**
As hard as it seems, apologize to those you have hurt. Accept responsibility to repair any damage done. Face it, fix it and forget it. Correcting what's wrong will earn you self-respect and the respect of others.

As a result of lack of self-control, tens of thousands of people every day do and say things that harm themselves and others. Are you one of those people? The lesson from Absalom is very clear. The loss of self-control can ultimately cost you everything, even your life. Is that a price you're willing to pay for your out-of-control behavior? Don't you think it's time to regain self-control?

INQUIRY-ACTION 9.1

MY BAGS ARE PACKED

It is time to embark on a trip to self-control. The bags you are to pack do not contain clothes. All you can take with you are those areas of your life you have under control. Areas not under control are "excess baggage." Note the "Things to Take" below and the "Excess Baggage" on the back side.

Things to Take

1.

2.

3.

INQUIRY-ACTION 9.1 (CONTINUED)

Excess Baggage

1. _____

_____

_____

2. _____

_____

_____

_____

3. _____

_____

_____

_____

_____
Signature

INQUIRY-ACTION 9.2

WORD GAMES

People try to pretend that their out-of-control behavior is really not a problem. Often they play word games to convince others, and themselves, that they're okay. Match the words with the games people play.

Words	Games
_____ 1. Minimizing	A. "If you were in my place, you'd do it, too."
_____ 2. Apathy	B. "Do you think I really care?"
_____ 3. Comparison	C. "I'll do something about it real soon."
_____ 4. Justification	D. "Like, I don't know I have a problem!"
_____ 5. Withdrawal	E. "I'm not going to talk about it."
_____ 6. Anger	F. "I don't do things like that."
_____ 7. Delay	G. "It's no big deal!"
_____ 8. Blaming	H. "If she didn't . . . ."
_____ 9. Humor	I. "I'm not as bad as . . . ."
_____ 10. Denial	J. "Get off my case!"

INQUIRY-ACTION 9.3

SIX STEPS TO SELF-CONTROL

Step 1:

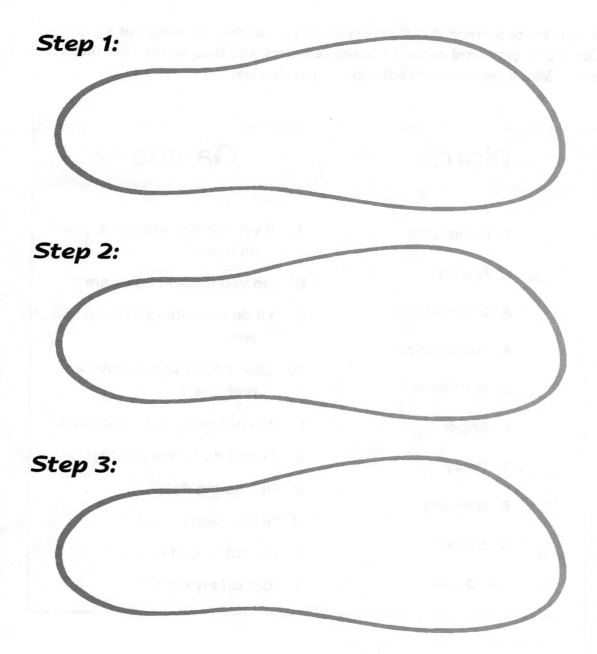

Step 2:

Step 3:

INQUIRY–ACTION 9.3 (CONTINUED)

Step 4:

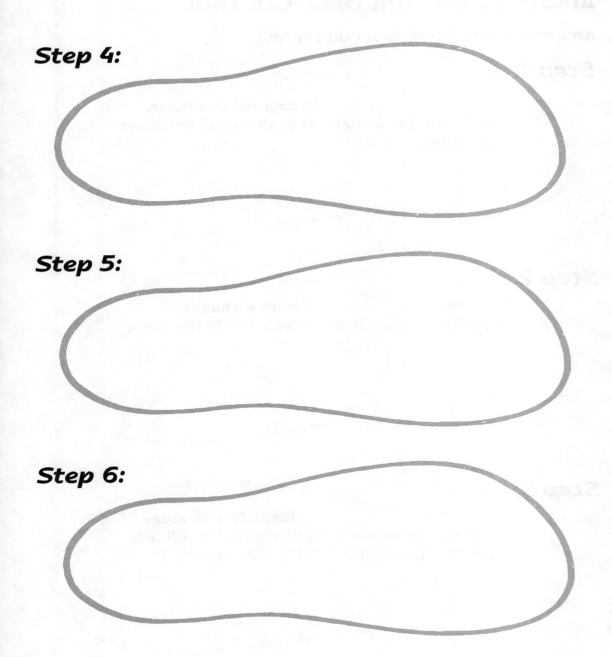

Step 5:

Step 6:

INQUIRY-ACTION 9.4

MASTER PLAN FOR SELF-CONTROL

Area over which I need to regain control: _____

Step 1:

Recognize weakness.
How do you know that this is an area of weakness in your life?

Step 2:

Desire a change.
Why do you want to make a change in this area?

Step 3:

Identify a strategy.
List specific actions you can take that will help you to regain self-control in this area.

INQUIRY–ACTION 9.4 (CONTINUED)

Step 4:

Accept the price.
Describe why it will be difficult for you to make a change in this area.

Step 5:

God's Spirit empowers.
Identify at least one passage of Scripture that gives you confidence that God will give you victory in this area.

Step 6:

Take action. Do what's right.
Will you do as you have promised yourself? What action will you take today to work on this area?

INQUIRY-ACTION 9.5

TITUS 2:11–13

Add back vowels, spaces and punctuation to the string of consonants listed in reverse order. Write the verses on the lines below.

t s r h c s s j r v s d n d g t r g r f g n r p p
s r l g d n p h d s s l b h t r f g n k l g t n
s r p h t n y l d g d n y l s t h g r y l r b s v
l d l h s w s t s l y l d l r w d n s s n l d g
n g n y n d t h t s g n h c t n m l l t d r p p
s h n t v l s s g n r b t h t d g f c r g h t r f

RUTH

Surviving a Terrible Loss

There are times in life that cannot be explained. Sometimes events bring great joy and happiness—on other occasions overwhelming grief and pain. One such tragedy occurred in the jungle of New Guinea.

It was a typical, lazy Sunday afternoon. No one was expecting the disaster that was about to strike the Steinkraus family—a disaster that would end the lives of these dedicated Wycliffe missionaries and their two children, Kerry and Kathy.

At exactly 3:00 p.m., an unexplainable natural disaster occurred. A huge section of the mountain on the opposite side of the river from the Steinkraus's house suddenly began to move. Within moments, it broke loose and began to plunge downward toward the river. This half-mile-wide section of earth crossed the river and covered the village with over ten feet of rocks and mud. The Steinkraus family was buried alive. There was no warning and no chance for escape. There was nothing that could be done.

Some villagers who were not in the path of the landslide survived. As a result of their first-hand report, family and friends in America soon learned of the terrible loss. The Western Union telegram read as follows:

```
┌─────────────────────────────────────────────────────┐
│            T E L E G R A M                            │
├─────────────────────────────────────────────────────┤
│   MARK 21/71  URGENT!  WALT AND VONNIE STEINKRAUS     │
│   AND CHILDREN BURIED IN VILLAGE BY LANDSLIDE         │
│   SUNDAY 21ST  STOP  PLEASE NOTIFY NEXT OF KIN  STOP  │
│   VONNIE'S FATHER HAS HEART CONDITION  STOP           │
└─────────────────────────────────────────────────────┘
```

The words of the telegram shocked everyone who knew this dedicated family. For years they had labored in remote parts of the world to faithfully translate the Bible into the native language. They had faced many hardships over the years, but God had graciously protected them. Now they were gone forever . . . their life's work unfinished . . . and two young children with no tomorrows. It seemed so wrong. Could this tragedy really be part of God's plan?

Sometimes God's plan doesn't make any sense to us at all.

Does the statement above bother you? Do you feel like you might be branded a "heretic" if you think that God's actions are unreasonable? Do people have a right to question why God allows something to happen? Does He cause such terrible disasters? Couldn't He have prevented them? Where is God when life hurts so much?

Take some comfort in knowing that you are not the first, or last, person to ask such questions. Also, know that the answers are not easy—they have perplexed humans from the ancient days of Job. They continue to haunt people who know that God is good and loving in all His ways (Psalm 145:17). Yet a terrible loss can again confront them with the age-old question: Why do bad things happen to good people?

The story of Ruth provides an example of how God's plan did not make earthly sense. A famine throughout Judah forced Elimelech to move to Moab in search of food. He took with him his wife Naomi and their two sons, Mahlon and Chilion.

After the family settled in Moab, the sons married women from that country. Mahlon married Ruth and Chilion married Orpah. But all three men died within ten years, leaving widows with no children. Since this was a male-dominated society, Naomi and her two daughters-in-law faced considerable hardship. Women without a father, husband or son to care for them could quickly become destitute; they had few rights.

Naomi, hearing that the famine in Judah had ended, decided to return to her homeland. Perhaps she thought relatives would take pity on her and give her a place to live. But they would certainly not take in all three women. She encouraged Ruth and Orpah to return home and look for other husbands among their own countrymen.

Orpah agreed and left. Ruth, however, absolutely refused to leave Naomi alone. "Wherever you go," Ruth insisted, "I will go, and wherever you lodge I will lodge; your people shall be my people, and your God my God" (Ruth 1:16).

By this time, Ruth had to be wondering about what was going on in her life. She had lost her husband and had no means of supporting herself. She had accepted Naomi's God as her own when she turned her back on the false idols of Moab. Now she was going to a foreign country to live among people whom she did not know.

In Ruth's life, God's plan must have seemed like a bad dream. It was a mystery that didn't make any sense at all. In spite of it all, she moved forward and trusted God. Why? Part of the answer lies in knowing that:

- God has a big plan.
- God sees the plan from beginning to end.
- God uses daily events, even disasters, to accomplish ultimate good.
- God loves you and will walk with you through hard times.
- God expects you to trust Him.

Ruth knew that God's plan could not be understood by mere mortals. His power is unlimited and His love eternal. She could only see what was happening right now. He could see forever. Knowing the beginning from the end, God's plan was perfect. Ruth's knowledge of God allowed her to face the terrible loss she experienced.

Still, in the midst of her pain and suffering, surely questions were going through her mind. Not only "Why?" but "What's next?" That is probably one of the most difficult questions we face as we experience a terrible loss. While a death, terminal illness or serious accident can devastate us, the fear of the unknown is almost more than we can bear.

The secret to overcoming a terrible loss is the realization that God's plan is beyond our understanding. We are earthbound, limited by time and human reasoning. Nothing limits God. Isaiah reminds us of this fact when he says,

> "For My thoughts are not your thoughts, nor are
> your ways My ways, says the Lord" (55:8).

No matter how terrible the tragedy or how difficult the pain, God is in control. Our responsibility is to accept His plan for our lives and trust Him to bring the peace and understanding that only He can provide. To assume that we can make sense out of a terrible loss or "make the pain go away" is to put ourselves in God's place. That's a pretty silly thought, isn't it?

Life can be like reading a mystery. Our problem is that we can't flip over to read the last chapter. We don't know how things are going to turn out! Fortunately, the story of Ruth helps us understand how God overcomes her loss. From the ashes of sorrow, hunger, danger and death come the wonderful joys of compassion, protection, love and a new life.

Trust God! What He did for Ruth, He will do for you!

INQUIRY-ACTION 10.1

A PERSONAL EXPERIENCE

1. In the space provided below, describe the most terrible loss you have ever experienced. If it is too difficult for you to tell about, describe what you believe would be the worst loss you would dread having to face.

_____

_____

_____

_____

_____

_____

_____

2. Write a couple of questions that come to your mind about God's control and nature in relation to bad things that happen.

_____

_____

_____

_____

_____

_____

_____

_____

INQUIRY–ACTION 10.1 (CONTINUED)

3. What is the best answer to your questions?

_____

_____

_____

_____

_____

_____

_____

4. What important things should you remember when facing times of terrible loss?

_____

_____

_____

_____

_____

_____

_____

_____

Name: _____

INQUIRY-ACTION 10.2

Famine

Foreign Wives

Widows

Poor People

Name Change

INQUIRY–ACTION 10.2 (CONTINUED)

Kinsman-Redeemer

Covering of Wings

Sandal

Lineage

INQUIRY–ACTION 10.3

LESSONS FROM THE BOOK OF RUTH: OVERCOMING A TERRIBLE LOSS

INQUIRY-ACTION 10.4

BEING A FRIEND WHEN BAD THINGS HAPPEN

INQUIRY–ACTION 10.5

PSALM 91:1–2

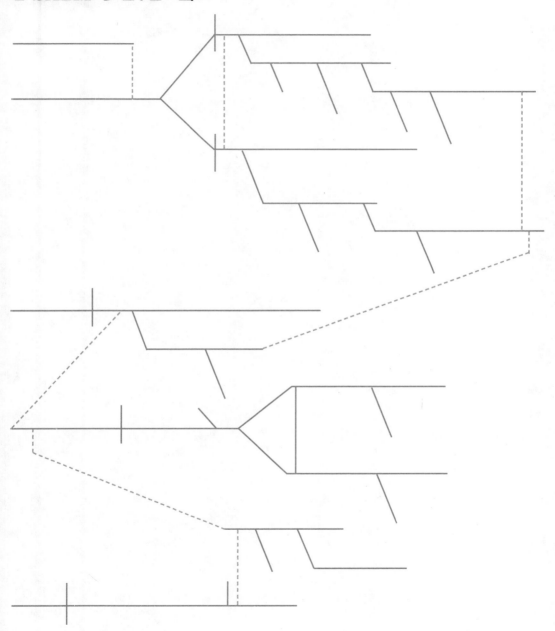

DAVID

Surviving Sin's Consequences

The ambulance rushed Phil to the hospital. Only moments before, he had been helping his wife construct a new wall unit in their home. But something went wrong. The heavy unit slipped, pinning his right hand to the floor. The pain was unbearable. As he learned later, it was the quick response of emergency personnel that saved his hand. An orthopedic surgeon had worked wonders. Phil's recovery, though long, was assured.

During a follow-up visit, the surgeon mentioned that his assistant would be treating Phil at the next visit. "I'm taking a much-needed vacation," he said. "I have been feeling pretty tired lately. I think my body is trying to tell me to take a rest. Besides, I have a little mole on my stomach that I'm having removed. It's no big deal."

A few weeks later Phil returned for his regular check-up and asked if the surgeon was having a good time on his vacation. Quietly, the assistant responded, "You mean you don't know? He died last week."

The shock was overwhelming. Phil had seen him less than a month before. "What happened?" he asked. Soon he heard the whole story. As planned, the surgeon had the mole removed. But during the operation, cancer was discovered. The cancer had spread throughout the doctor's body. There was nothing more that could be done. It was only a matter of days before he died. The only warning had been the little mole.

Think about it for a moment. Sin is a lot like that little mole. It starts small, sometimes hardly noticeable. Many times, the sin is so well hidden that no one really knows how much devastation it is actually causing. Over a period of time, it drains our spiritual energy, just like cancer destroys the body. Before long, our spiritual defenses can become so weakened that the sin spreads at even a faster pace.

The consequences of sin, like a cancer, are devastating. Unless the sin is stopped, it will affect everything a person does. There will be no recovery.

David's sin with Bathsheba certainly illustrates how sin can multiply. At the same time, David shows us that by God's grace, recovery from the consequences of sin is possible.

It was bad enough that David had committed adultery with Bathsheba. But when he learned that she was expecting a child, he knew that his sin would become known throughout the kingdom. His messengers knew that they had been together (2 Samuel 11:4) and everyone knew that her husband, Uriah the Hittite, was away at war. It would be obvious that David was the father of the unborn child.

As is always true, sin leads to more sin. David sent for Uriah, encouraging him to take a much-needed rest. David believed that if Uriah returned home, he would sleep with his wife. Then, thought David, Uriah would not be suspicious when he learned a baby was on the way.

Uriah did not comply with David's plan. Knowing that his troops were living in tents near the battlefield, Uriah did not believe it was right for him to enjoy the comforts of his home. Therefore, he slept at the door of the king's house (2 Samuel 11:9).

David devised a new plan. He sent word to his commander, Joab, to place Uriah in the forefront of the hottest battle. Joab was then instructed to pull back his troops, leaving Uriah unprotected (2 Samuel 11:15). David was confident that Uriah would become a casualty of war.

This time David's plan worked. When Bathsheba learned of Uriah's death, she mourned for him. After her time of mourning had ended, David married her. It looked as if David had successfully covered his sins and they would live happily ever after. Or would they?

God sees all. David had been a man "after God's own heart." He would not allow David to sin without facing its consequences. "Then the Lord sent Nathan to David" (2 Samuel 12:1).

> "Why have you despised the commandment of the
> Lord, to do evil in His sight? You have killed Uriah the
> Hittite with the sword; you have taken his wife to be your
> wife, and have killed him with the sword of the people
> of Ammon" (2 Samuel 12:9).

The secret was out. What had begun as a single, secret sin had multiplied to include other sins. Initially only two people had been involved. Now the lives of many people were affected. Was it possible for David to recover from the consequences of his sin? The answer is clearly, "Yes"!

Psalm 51 was written by David shortly after Nathan the prophet confronted him. From this Psalm we can learn how it is possible to recover from the consequences of sin.

Recovery begins with confession (verse 3). Unless we are willing to admit to our sins, there is no hope of recovery.

Recovery continues with cleansing (verse 7). Only God can forgive our sins, cleanse us and make us "whiter than snow." This wonderful promise is only for those who first confess their sins.

Recovery includes a new direction (verse 10). Part of the recovery process requires turning our backs on sin and walking in righteousness. God gives this new direction by renewing a right spirit in the life of the believer.

Recovery results in restored joy (verse 12). As the result of confessed sin, a cleansed life and a new direction, David again experienced the joy of the Lord. In spite of his terrible sins, David could once again enjoy God's many blessings.

Recovery was possible because of God's mercy. David's sins were not only forgiven, his guilt was taken away. As a result of God's mercy and loving kindness (verse 1), He relieved David from the misery of guilt.

What kind of unconfessed sin are you living with right now? Maybe you are not yet suffering from the consequences of your sin—but you will! Then again, maybe you are already paying the price for what you have done.

Here's a simple question: "Do you want to continue in your sin, or do you want to recover from its consequences?" David tried to hide his sin, and failed. You will too. Recovery begins with confession. Are you ready to take that first step?

INQUIRY–ACTION 11.1

Certificate of Commendation

Awarded to

David

**For Attitudes and Actions Which Have Earned
Respect Throughout All Generations**

_____ _____

_____ _____

_____ _____

_____ _____

_____ _____

_____ _____

*"He raised up for them David as king,
to whom also He gave testimony and said,
'I have found David the son of Jesse, a man after
My own heart, who will do all My will'." (Acts 13:22)*

INQUIRY-ACTION 11.2

THE NATURE AND EFFECTS OF SIN

2 Samuel 11:1–12:14

①

②

③

④

⑤

⑥

INQUIRY–ACTION 11.2 (CONTINUED)

❼

❽

❾

❿

⓫

⓬

INQUIRY-ACTION 11.3

DAVID'S PATHWAY TO RECOVERY

As you read Psalm 51, identify the steps David felt were necessary in order to recover from the consequences of sin.

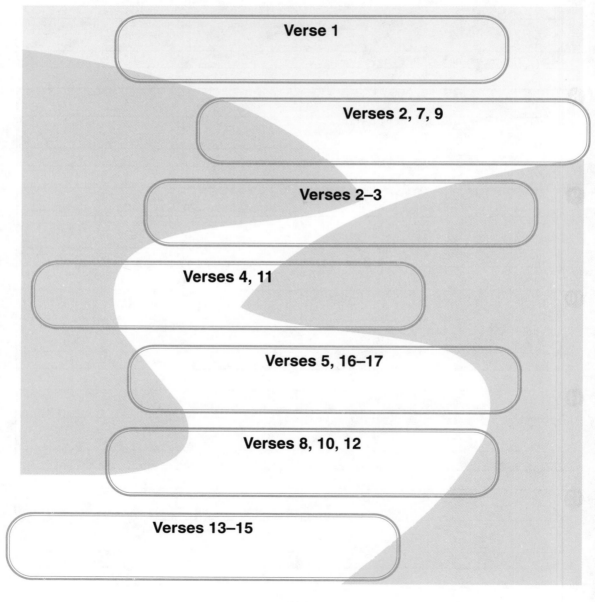

Verse 1

Verses 2, 7, 9

Verses 2–3

Verses 4, 11

Verses 5, 16–17

Verses 8, 10, 12

Verses 13–15

INQUIRY-ACTION 11.4

THE QUESTION OF SIN

1. How did sin originate? _____
_____

2. What is sin? _____
_____

3. Who sins?_____
_____

4. Why do people, in general, resist calling wrongdoing sin? _____
_____
_____

5. What is the difference between temptation and sin? _____
_____
_____

6. What is the final outcome of sin? _____
_____

7. What is God's answer for sin? _____
_____

8. What should a Christian do who has sinned? _____
_____

INQUIRY-ACTION 11.5

PSALM 51:10–12

Use the bank of nouns and verbs to help you write the verses. The numerals indicate the number of words that must be added after the words provided.

Create ₄
heart ₁
God ₁
renew ₂
spirit ₂
cast ₄
presence ₃
take ₂
Spirit ₂
Restore ₃
joy ₂
salvation ₁
uphold ₄
Spirit

SAMSON

Surviving Irresponsible Behavior

Do you have a friend who just seems terribly irresponsible? Focused on having fun and enjoying life, he never counts the cost of his actions. Sometimes guilty of devious pranks or deliberate revenge; sometimes unintentional remarks or rash reactions—either way he can spin out of control and is likely to make a fool of himself, and you too.

His parents may have already sought medical help for an attention deficit disorder (ADD) or hyperactivity. Perhaps the teachers blame his parents for spoiling him and giving in to his demands. Your other friends caution, "Hang around him very long and you're sure to get into trouble."

Brad was that kind of kid. The comments on his report cards through the years included "unfocused, disorganized, doesn't follow through, immature, careless, never thinks ahead, loses control, gullible, tries to fit in with the wrong crowd, fails to live up to his potential." Jane was another one. Trying not to offend, her fifth-grade teacher wrote, "Jane continues to need to learn to use her excess energy in more positive ways." Her parents understood the coded message: she's bouncing off the walls and driving the teacher crazy.

Are such kids doomed to a life of misery and failure? Is there no hope? Actually, both Brad and Jane are college graduates and serve the Lord as missionaries; one is in a former communist state in Eastern Europe and the other is a pilot in the jungles of South America. What happened to change their life directions? One simple decision—to take responsibility.

It happened when they were about your age. In serious commitment to the Lord, each faced the fact that choices lead to actions, and actions have consequences.

If they had persisted in their poor judgments and lack of self-control, the results could have been disastrous. Instead, they began to consciously consider their words and behaviors. They looked at potential consequences before making decisions. They became conscientious in completing tasks and doing their best.

Sure, there were setbacks. Habits are hard to break. It's easy to speak without thinking. It's natural to lose your temper. The difference was their acceptance of personal responsibility. What they did in life was up to them, not their parents or teachers. Commitment came from their hearts, not the outward enforcement of rules. Control became self-control.

The story of Samson in the book of Judges is probably one of the most familiar stories of the Bible. A child of parents barren until old age, he was an answer to prayer and destined to greatness as a leader to free the Israelites from the oppression of the Philistines. No young man ever had better opportunities or more potential. Yet, it all went down the drain.

Time after time he proved himself to be physically strong but character challenged. Foolish, deceitful, rash, without moral restraint, Samson made one bad decision after another. As a Nazirite, he vowed to avoid finding pleasure in the world (signified by not drinking wine), to be identified with God (signified by not cutting his hair), and to be committed to bring life and healing to the nation (signified by never touching any dead body). Samson violated every vow. The result was disgrace and failure.

Samson's irresponsibility and poor judgment are illustrated in his choice of a life mate. In the first incident, Samson certainly thought that he was "in love" with the woman in Timnath (Judges 14–15). As a result of what he saw, he demanded that his parents get her for him as his wife.

As you read the first few verses of Judges 14, you realize that Samson's process for selecting a mate had a number of "warning signs" of irresponsibility. The first warning sign was that she was a Philistine. She believed in a pagan god, while he trusted in the God of Israel. He disobeyed the clear command of God that forbade such intermarriages.

The second warning sign was the difference in family and cultural backgrounds. The Philistines and Israelites had been at war for centuries. Not only were they enemies, their values and priorities were drastically different. The Philistines were warriors. The Israelites were shepherds. Conquering other nations was high priority for the Philistines. The Israelites were more concerned with establishing strong families and raising their children to know and love God. Samson's job was to free his people from their oppression. Instead of assembling an army, he became one of the oppressors.

A third warning sign was Samson's refusal to take the counsel of his parents. He was so blinded by what he thought was love, that he ignored their advice. Like all parents, they wanted only what was best for their child. They lovingly tried to redirect Samson's life, but he would not listen to the two people who loved him most.

The result of Samson's selection was a disaster. The woman from Timnath deceived him (Judges 14:15–17) and eventually married someone else (Judges 15:1–2). As a result of her deception, Samson took revenge on 30 men of Ashkelon (Judges 14:19), destroyed the crops of the Philistines (Judges 15:3–5) and then killed an additional 1,000 Philistine men (Judges 15:14–20). The Philistines, angered by what Samson had done, killed both the woman from Timnath and her father.

It is Samson's encounter with Delilah that demonstrates his total loss of self-control. Once again, his physical passion caused him to "fall in love" with a Philistine woman. But this was not just any Philistine woman. She was allied closely with Israel's enemies to destroy Samson.

She repeatedly asked Samson to reveal the secret of his strength. Knowing that she was working with the Philistine leaders, he lied to her about the source of his strength. Finally, according to Judges 16:16, her crying and begging became so intense that Samson was aggravated to death. He gave in and told her the true source of his strength. As a result, Samson was captured, tortured and ultimately died in one last cataclysmic collapse of the Philistine temple.

From the woman at Timnath to Delilah, Samson's decisions were driven by his physical passions. Although he lived centuries ago, his story still clearly reminds us of how not to select a life mate. Samson ignored the "warning signs" that clearly marked the problems he would face.

A few miles north of San Diego there is a checkpoint where the U.S. Immigration and Naturalization Services tries to spot cars hiding illegal aliens and transporting them across the border from Mexico to the United States. Signs along the freeway warn drivers about the upcoming inspection and caution them to slow down.

There is always a backup of traffic caused by cars moving through the inspection area. As the cars slowly pass the agents, they are waved through to their final destination. Occasionally a car will be stopped and the driver asked to park in a reserved area. Special agents are then called to carefully inspect every part of the vehicle.

How do the agents determine which cars will be inspected and which cars will be allowed to proceed? Their decisions are based upon whether or not the cars, or their passengers, exhibit certain characteristics. They have learned to look for certain "signs" which indicate that illegal aliens might be present.

There are many "signs" along the pathway of life. Some are warning signs, while others point us in the right direction. Irresponsible or responsible? Good judgment or poor?   Which way are the signs of your life pointed?

Inquiry-Action 12.1

Proverbs

1. 14:9 _____

2. 1:7; 15:2 _____

3. 13:1; 17:25 _____

4. 9:13; 10:14 _____

5. 24:9; 14:7 _____

6. 22:10 _____

7. 20:3; 29:9 _____

8. 21:24; 12:15 _____

9. 12:16; 14:16 _____

10. 14:8 _____

11. 10:8; 19:29 _____

12. 9:6; 10:21 _____

INQUIRY-ACTION 12.2

WALKING GOD'S WAY — PSALM 37

Verse 5	*Commit to the Lord.*

Verses 1, 7 and 34	*Don't fret.*

Verses 8 and 37	*Control your anger.*

INQUIRY–ACTION 12.2 (CONTINUED)

Verses 30–31	*Watch your words.*

Verses 3–4 and 27–28	*Do right.*

Verses 23–24 and 39	*Depend on the Lord.*

INQUIRY–ACTION 12.3

PROVERBS 37:3–5

Use the words provided and complete the phrase in order to write the verses.

Trust	_____
and	_____
Dwell	_____
and	_____
Delight	_____
in	_____
And	_____
the	_____
Commit	_____
to	_____
Trust	_____
and	_____

PHILEMON

Surviving Personal Conflicts

Right now, this very minute, with whom are you having conflict? Is it a member of your family, one of your friends or someone you hardly know? Has the conflict become so intense that it consumes your thinking? Is the emotion from this conflict spilling over and affecting the lives of others around you?

Just one more question: Do you want revenge, or resolution?

Last summer Jack and Chuck carefully worked out all the details. Miss Brown, their school principal, would be away for a month visiting her nephew on the mission field. She asked for a couple of responsible students to care for her plants during her absence. Working around family vacation schedules, Jack was to water plants during the first two weeks and Chuck would water them during the last two weeks. Miss Brown paid them twenty dollars up front and promised twenty more when she returned. The first payment was promptly split, and spent, by the two friends.

All went as planned until the third week. Jack and his family were out of town. Without any prior notice, Chuck's uncle showed up one evening and invited him to ride in his 18-wheeler to make a delivery to the docks in New Orleans. The offer was too good to turn down, but in his excitement Chuck failed to find someone to cover his responsibilities at Miss Brown's. By the next day, and the day after, either Chuck was not near a telephone or the friends he called were not home.

After unloading cargo at the docks, Chuck's uncle was delayed in picking up the return cargo. That left some free time to visit the Aquarium of the Americas and ride an old-fashioned riverboat. It was all great fun, especially the IMAX 3-D film

Into the Deep. Chuck could hardly wait to tell Jack how you could almost touch the fish swimming past your head. But, there it was! Every thought of Jack brought back that sinking sensation of the neglected duties at home. His best hope was that the plants would weather the dry spell and, with a little extra attention, would recover before Miss Brown's return.

Unfortunately, Chuck did not have an opportunity to see if his plan would work. By the time his uncle dropped him at home, Miss Brown had already found her plants—some salvageable, others dry and brown. Her first call had been to Jack's mom; the second had been to his mom. Disbelief. Shock. Disappointment. Embarrassment. Anger. A firm agreement that both boys should learn their lesson. Jack's dad said, "Whoever dances, pays the piper." The boys didn't know exactly what that meant, but were soon to find out.

Not only did Miss Brown not pay the last twenty dollars, she demanded a return of the first twenty. What's more, Jack and Chuck were to replace all the plants that died due to the lack of water. It meant that all of their allowances, added to money earned from odd jobs and extra chores, would barely pay the tab by the time school started. And neither boy liked the idea of starting school with Miss Brown still upset over her plants. After all, having the principal mad at you could be the "kiss of death."

About a week later, Chuck took the photographs and souvenirs from his New Orleans' trip over to Jack's. Even with all the trouble, he was still super excited and could hardly wait to share his experiences. He was not prepared for Jack's reaction. "I can't believe you did such a stupid thing. It's all your fault, but I'm the one being punished. It's not fair! I did my part. You're the one who messed up. You're the one who ought to pay, not me!"

Nothing Chuck said, or did, made any difference. He even offered to work extra and pay more, but it didn't matter. A friendship that started in fourth grade had suddenly come to an end. What was worse—Chuck felt that they were becoming enemies. Jack complained about the situation to everyone, making sure people understood it was all Chuck's fault.

Things were no better after school started. Sure, the debt was paid and Miss Brown didn't hold it against them, but Jack seemed delighted to turn their friends against Chuck. It wasn't just the plants. Jack was telling things shared in the confidence of friendship. Silly things. Hurtful things. Things that boys talk about while camping or dangling their feet in the water of the creek.

Before long, Chuck started matching story for story, and their friends, especially the girls, buzzed between the two carrying the latest tales. As their anger grew, so did their competition. Each one trying to outdo the other led to conflicts, especially in physical education class. The boiling caldron finally erupted into a shoving-pushing contest while the teacher's back was turned.

"Fighting automatically results in a three-day suspension plus every grade lowered by one letter for the semester," Miss Brown explained to their parents. Jack and Chuck could only stare silently at the floor.

It is clear that conflict has the ability to destroy every relationship that it touches. That is why the Scripture so clearly says, "But if you bite and devour one another, beware lest you be consumed by one another" (Galatians 5:15).

The Book of Philemon provides a classic example of how to deal with conflict. According to Acts 19:8–10, Paul spent more than two years preaching in Ephesus. One of his converts was a wealthy man from Colosse named Philemon. As a result of his new faith, Philemon returned home to share the gospel with his family and friends. Many Bible scholars believe that the letter to the Colossians was written to the church started in his home.

Like most wealthy citizens of the Roman empire, Philemon owned slaves. One of Philemon's slaves was named Onesimus. It is not known whether Onesimus was a thief who was about to be caught or just wanted his freedom. Whatever the reason, he ran away. Under the laws of that day, he could have been killed or imprisoned for life if caught.

Several years later, Onesimus was in Rome and met Paul. As a result, he became a Christian. It is certain that Onesimus told Paul about his past.

Paul now faced a dilemma. Should he advise Onesimus to remain in Rome where he would be safe? Or should he return the runaway slave to his master as required by law? If Onesimus returned, he could be severely punished.

Paul decided that the right thing to do was to return Onesimus to Philemon. Paul prepared three letters—one each for the believers in Colosse and Laodicea and a personal letter to Philemon. It was in his letter to Philemon that Paul sought to resolve the conflict that existed between Philemon and Onesimus. Paul's letter provides a number of important lessons on how to overcome differences and bring healing in times of conflict.

The most important lesson from the Book of Philemon is that no matter what has happened, there is always an opportunity for reconciliation. After a person has accepted Jesus Christ as Savior, there is a "second chance" to make things right. Paul wanted Philemon to remember what he had been like before accepting Christ. Now Paul was asking Philemon to also give Onesimus a second chance.

A second important lesson is illustrated in verses 17–19. Paul told Philemon that "if" Onesimus owed anything, he should send Paul the bill for it. In other words, Paul was saying "Let me pick up the tab." Paul volunteered to pay for the loss if Philemon was unwilling simply to forgive it.

Paul's words remind us that Jesus Christ willingly paid the price for our sins by dying on the Cross. Philemon owed Paul a great spiritual debt. After all, his salvation was due to Paul's ministry in Ephesus. Paul asked Philemon to consider this debt in balance to Onesimus' debt. To cancel one meant the other was canceled also.

When Christ commands us to forgive others as He has forgiven us, the same balance sheet exists. The wrongs of others toward you can never match your wrongs against the Lord. In canceling your great debt, He expects you, in turn, to forgive the wrongs of others.

Take a moment to consider how these two lessons apply in your life. Probably with very little difficulty, you could list a number of conflicts that have caused you pain. Think about the individuals involved in those conflicts and decide whether you want resolution, or revenge?

It would have been easy for Philemon to justify revenge. After all, Onesimus was his property. Onesimus had run away and probably stolen from him. Onesimus embarrassed him in front of other slave owners. His absence cost Philemon the wages of others needed to perform his duties.

But Paul reminded Philemon that Onesimus should be given a second chance. Believers should treat each other differently from those who do not know Jesus Christ as Savior. Onesimus should be treated as a brother—not as an enemy!

Are you willing to forgive those who have caused you pain during times of conflict? According to Paul's instruction in Philemon, that is your responsibility as a believer.

Maybe you are aware of a conflict that does not directly involve you. That is where the second lesson becomes very important. From Paul's example we should learn to be willing to "pick up the tab." In other words, in order to help resolve conflicts between others, we are willing to personally give the necessary resources (money, time, possessions, etc.) to bring peace. That is the true test of spiritual maturity and conflict resolution.

Remember, a conflict is an emotional collision. It is open and hostile opposition that results from different viewpoints. The greater the difference, the more severe the collision.

There are no quick, easy solutions to complex conflicts. However, there is one fact about conflicts that stands out from all the rest. Unless the people involved are willing to resolve the conflict, the pain will only become greater. The conflict will never resolve itself.

If you are involved in a conflict, are you willing to take the first step to resolve the problem? Somebody has to take the first step. It might as well be you. That is clearly what Jesus wants you to do.

Inquiry–Action 13.1

Philemon

The Characters		
Philemon	**Onesimus**	**Paul**
The Problems Faced		

INQUIRY-ACTION 13.1 (CONTINUED)

Outline
The Applause –
The Appeal –
The Approval –

Lessons for Life

Inquiry-Action 13.2

Learning from Paul's Example

Approach to Conflict Resolution

1. *Affirm the relationship.*

2. *Focus on the positive first.*

3. *Be willing to make a personal commitment.*

4. *Work on a mutual solution.*

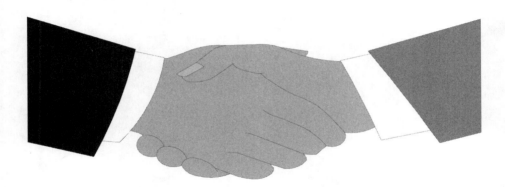

INQUIRY-ACTION 13.3

U O Me!

Ledger of _____

Due from _____

Reimbursement for _____

_____

Mark all that apply:

☐ I am willing to give up the U O Me's.

☐ I will seek God's forgiveness for my wrongdoing in this conflict.

☐ I will seek to forgive the person for his/her wrongdoing in this conflict.

☐ I will stop my negative actions. This includes criticism, repeating the story, placing blame and getting support from my friends.

☐ I will look for opportunities to rebuild the relationship. I understand that I may need to apologize. I will be positive in my actions and words.

☐ I understand that the person may not be ready to resolve the conflict and may not return my kindness. That's okay. Either way, I will do right because that's what God expects.

INQUIRY-ACTION 13.3 (CONTINUED)

☐ I will continue to seek a mutual solution that will end this conflict at some future time.

My Prayer

_____

_____

_____

_____

_____

_____

_____

_____

Signature

_____

Date

INQUIRY-ACTION 13.4

GALATIANS 5:13–15

Circle the words in the Word Find and write the verses on the lines below.

```
L L A H S U M M E D I N D U L L O T H E R B B Y
C A L L D C O M M A N D M E N T L N A U R O U T
Y M E N E O T Y B N D P Y T R E B I L O E H T R
O R C O N S U M E D U N O B E B Y N W Y H O D E
U P E E K T U O F U L F I L L E D O O S T N R B
W U P B U E H D A O G T H C T A W U E T A I A I
D E Y O R T S E D N E I G H B O R L F O R S W L
T O B I R H W E I E H C A E R S F E N I D N E L
U B T E A T H R O U G H L D E S R E H T O R B A
B N P L W L U F N I S A L L T E E R U T A N D O
E P L E V O L N S N H E F H H B E E R U O V E D
O S E R V E R A I E S U I T R V O W E L G N I S
H C A E I V V D W T E S T O E P R E H T O N A E
S A D W F O R A U O Y E H N N D E L L A C A L L
```

_____

_____

_____

_____

_____

Find the words in the word find and write the verses on the lines below.

JOASH

Surviving Overwhelming Responsibility

"He was indeed, in every sense of the words, a wise, a good and a great man . . . on the whole, his character was, in its mass, perfect . . . it may truly be said that never did nature and fortune combine more perfectly to make a man great . . . ."

These were the words of Thomas Jefferson, written in praise of his friend, George Washington, after Washington's death on December 14, 1799. George Washington, a man who faced overwhelming responsibility, gave God the glory for his ability to accomplish the great tasks before him.

George Washington has remained one of the most admired men in America's history. His name appears on schools, cities, streets, counties, buildings, parks and the nation's capital. He is the only president to have a state named after him. Why is this man so richly honored by a nation? The following "snapshots" of his life will provide the answer.

The French and Indian War. Washington received a godly heritage from his mother. When leaving home to serve in the military, she reminded him, "Remember that God is our only sure trust. Neglect not the duty of secret prayer." At the age of 20 he was given a commission in the Virginia militia. He rose rapidly through the ranks of the military to the level of Colonel. The drums of war were beating all along the East Coast as the French and British tried to take firm control of these new colonies. His brilliant command of troops, and ability to predict British strategy, earned him respect throughout the young nation. Later, he would be given a position of leadership in the Continental Army.

Conflict with the British. Right from the beginning, George Washington was involved in the broiling revolution against the British crown. He took part in the meetings of the Continental Congress and was unanimously elected first commander-in-chief of the newly-formed Continental Army. Washington's troops eventually defeated the British at Yorktown, ending British rule of the colonies. Commenting on his victories, a pastor noted, "George Washington respects God's Word, believes in the atonement through Christ, and bears himself in humility and gentleness. Therefore, the Lord God has also singularly, yea marvelously, preserved him from harm in the midst of countless perils."

Rejection of a Monarchy. At the conclusion of the war, Washington's popularity was so great that he was asked to become king of the colonies. Washington quickly refused and returned to his Virginia home. He firmly believed that the type of rule in England should not be repeated in the colonies. Through his leadership, the common motto of the American colonies was "No king but King Jesus!"

President of the Constitutional Convention. Five years after the conclusion of the war, a Constitutional Convention was called to replace the Articles of Confederation. Elected as president of the Constitutional Convention, Washington guided the work of the convention. A year later, states had approved the Constitution and the government was formed. The United States of America, the greatest democracy in the world, had become a reality.

President of the United States. The most important "snapshot" of Washington's life was still to come. Now that the nation was formed, it needed a leader. George Washington was elected as the first president of the United States. He accepted one of the most overwhelming of all responsibilities. It would be his task to carry out the great principles of the newly written Constitution and draw together a nation of people under a new form of government.

When George Washington accepted the responsibility of president, he also acknowledged God's direction in his life and in the formation of the nation. "Let my heart, therefore, gracious God, be so affected with the glory and majesty of You that I may not do mine own works, but wait on Thee, and discharge those weighty duties which Thou requirest of me."

Shortly after his inauguration, he challenged the country with these words: "Let us unite, therefore, in imploring the Supreme Ruler of nations, to spread his holy protection over these United States; to turn the machinations of the wicked to the confirming of our constitutions; to enable us at all times to root out internal sedition, and put invasion to flight; to perpetuate to our country that prosperity, which His goodness has already conferred, and to verify the anticipation of this government being a safeguard to humans rights."

Facing responsibility is a daily part of life. Parents have responsibilities at home, church and work that must be fulfilled each week. Students have responsibilities at home and the responsibility to complete their lessons and conduct themselves properly in school. It was no different in George Washington's day. Throughout his life he faced the daily responsibilities of leading our nation.

Everyone lives with daily responsibilities. However, at various times we must accept responsibilities that can be overwhelming, responsibilities that far outweigh our natural strength. These require an extra measure of confidence, conviction and courage. George Washington faced his as an adult. Pierre DuPont became father to his nine brothers and sisters at age fourteen. For Joash, overwhelming responsibility was thrust upon him at the age of seven.

It was only by God's protection that Joash was even able to reach the age of seven. When he was one year old, his grandmother (Athaliah) tried to kill every heir to the throne so that she could become queen. Joash was rescued by an aunt, Jehosheba, and hidden by Jehoiada the high priest.

Athaliah, a daughter of Jezebel, spent the next six years spreading pagan Baal worship throughout the land. However, during these same six years, Jehoiada was preparing Joash for the tremendous responsibilities that he would soon face.

When Joash reached his seventh birthday, Jehoiada brought him out of hiding and crowned him the ninth king of Judah. The people rejoiced! The celebration was so loud that Athaliah ran to see what was happening. Realizing that Joash had been crowned king, she cried, "Treason, Treason!" Jehoiada ordered the guards to seize her. Although she tried to escape, she was caught and executed.

As the youngest king in Judah's history, Joash now faced an overwhelming responsibility. Not only did he lack the maturity and experience to be king, but he also had to remove the Baal worship that existed throughout his country. According to the Bible, Joash . . .

. . . appointed Jehoiada, the high priest, as his advisor.
. . . destroyed the religious articles imported by Athaliah.
. . . had Mattan, the Baal priest, killed.
. . . re-established worship as required by the Mosaic Law.
. . . repaired the Temple.

These were great challenges. How was Joash able to have the confidence, conviction and courage to handle the overwhelming responsibility he faced? While the answer to this question is not specifically given, the following principles can be concluded from the story.

Principle 1: *Know God and His Word.*
During the six years that Athaliah was spreading pagan Baal worship, Joash was learning about God from Jehoiada. Successfully handling overwhelming responsibility always begins with knowing God and obeying His Word.

Principle 2: *Accept your circumstances as ordained of God.*
Joash did not seek to be king. However, that was his appointment in life. We often do not have a choice in our life circumstances. When required, we must accept the unexpected responsibilities thrust on us.

Principle 3: Follow God's will.

"The steps of a good man are ordered by the Lord: and He delights in his way" (Psalm 37:23). Whatever our life circumstances, we must react according to what God wants to accomplish through us. God's will for Joash was to remove Baal worship and restore the worship of the true God. If we follow His will, we will be able to handle any overwhelming responsibility we face.

Principle 4: Seek help.

The first action Joash took when he became king was to appoint Jehoiada as his advisor. He knew that in his own ability he would be unable to accomplish what had to be done. Don't be afraid to ask for help when you need it.

Principle 5: Take the long view.

Great accomplishments never happen overnight. It took years to remove the Baal idols from the land. Handling the overwhelming responsibilities you face will also require "taking the long view." Don't give up. Don't look for the easy way out. Take one day at a time. Persist in doing what you are responsible to do.

Principle 6: Maintain your relationship with the Lord.

Never let the stress of the responsibility cause you to neglect your personal commitment to the Lord. Your daily time of prayer and communion with God will give you the strength to do what is right that day.

Although you have probably never had responsibilities as enormous as those faced by George Washington or young King Joash, you may face responsibilities even greater than these in the coming years. At the same time, the responsibilities you face today may seem overwhelming. Either way, with God's help, you can handle any responsibility that comes your way. Throughout history, men and women have trusted God when faced with overwhelming responsibility. Just as He has been faithful to them, He will be faithful to you.

INQUIRY-ACTION 14.1

FULFILLING RESPONSIBILITY LIKE A . . .

Lessons to Be Learned _____

_____

_____

_____

_____

INQUIRY–ACTION 14.1 (CONTINUED)

Lessons to Be Learned _____

_____

_____

_____

_____

INQUIRY-ACTION 14.2

WHEN RESPONSIBILITIES SEEM OVERWHELMING

Principle 1: Know God and His Word.

Principle 2: _____ your _____ as ordained of God.

Principle 3: _____ God's will.

Principle 4: _____ help.

Principle 5: _____ the _____ view.

Principle 6: _____ your _____ with the Lord.

INQUIRY-ACTION 14.3

2 THESSALONIANS 2:15–17

JOSEPH

Surviving Sibling Rivalry

The Bible, especially the Old Testament, has much to say about warfare and weapons. Since wars during Bible times were fought on land, foot soldiers battled each other in hand-to-hand combat. The bow was usually the first weapon of choice fired in an open-field battle because the archers of the attacking armies could fire arrows from long distances.

Simple bows, composed of a piece of wood and string, were easy to make. However, a bow was of no use without an arrow, usually made with a stone or piece of metal attached to a long shaft of wood. When struck by an arrow, the victim was either killed immediately or severely injured. In the hands of a capable archer, the bow and arrow was a formidable weapon.

An arrow is not always an instrument of warfare. Sometimes it is described in figurative language. For example, have you ever seen pictures of Cupid with his bow and arrow? Prior to Valentine's Day, his picture appears in all of the gift and card shops. As the story goes, when you are shot by one of his arrows you will fall in love. It's all a make-believe game, but it gives you an idea of how the arrow has come to mean more than a weapon of war.

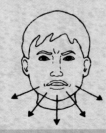

For the next few minutes, think about all of the different ways that brothers and sisters can mistreat each other. Ridicule, gossip, teasing, physical abuse, tattling, rejection and criticism are just a few examples. Have you ever thought about how these forms of sibling rivalry are like arrows? For example, when an

older sibling ridicules you, do the words cause pain and hurt? Certainly, they do.
Even though you have not been physically attacked, you suffer emotionally, deep in
your heart.

Unfortunately, these arrows of mistreatment—the taunts and teasing of sibling
rivalry—are common. Even in Christian families, brothers and sisters think nothing
of hurting each other with their words and actions. These arrows hurt! They always
have. The story of Joseph, son of Jacob, is a good illustration.

Joseph was cruelly treated by his brothers. According to Genesis 37, his brothers
hated him, envied him, conspired to kill him, cast him into a pit, sold him into
slavery and then lied about it to their father. These arrows wounded Joseph deeply.
He did not expect his own flesh and blood to mistreat him in this way.

How do you respond when the arrows of sibling rivalry are hurled at you? Before
you answer that question, take another look at Joseph's life. Read Genesis 39–41
and pay close attention to how Joseph DID NOT respond to his brothers' mistreatment. Notice that he did not become angry or curse his brothers. Neither did he
strike back in revenge. He did not become bitter in his situation. And, most
importantly, he did not blame God.

Years later, when Joseph had risen to a position of great importance in Egypt, he
saw his brothers again. This time the circumstances were very different. Joseph
was now the master of all of Pharaoh's house. He was both wealthy and powerful.
In contrast, Joseph's brothers had come to beg for food because there was a
famine in Israel. They were poor and helpless; their families were on the brink of
starvation.

Yet Joseph did not use his royal position to punish his brothers for what they had
done to him years ago. Much to their surprise, he spoke to them kindly. Joseph
told his brothers that their mistreatment of him was part of God's plan to preserve
the nation. Genesis 45:7–8a records Joseph's words.

> *"And God sent me before you to preserve a posterity for you in the
> earth, and to save your lives by a great deliverance. So it was not
> you who sent me here, but God."*

Now, think again about the question asked a few moments ago. How do you respond when the arrows of sibling rivalry are hurled at you? If you're not careful, criticism, ridicule, gossip—and all of the other arrows—will hurt you so deeply that you will either respond in anger or believe the lies and give up. This is not the way to respond.

When the arrows of sibling rivalry come your way, use them as an opportunity to deepen your character and faith. Remember, even when you are mistreated, God is always in absolute control. It was his attitude of confidence in God that enabled Joseph to withstand the hatred and mistreatment of his brothers.

Like it or not, God has placed you in the exact family He wants you to have. Whether ideal or plagued with problems similar to Joseph's, your family provides the most enduring relationships of life. Sure there are times of preferential treatment. Brothers and sisters squabble, make up, can't stand each other then become best friends, all on a regular basis. In the midst of it, your single most important decision is a choice of attitude.

Will you be bitter? or better!

The next time you are caught in the crossfire of sibling rivalry, take control of the situation by having the right attitude. Respond as Joseph did by . . .

> . . . forgiving those who mistreat you.
> . . . acknowledging that God is in complete control.
> . . . rejoicing that you are a child of God and a part of His plan.

Use the arrows of sibling rivalry that are hurled at you to strengthen your character and focus your attention upon the God who loves you. This attitude will ultimately give you the victory.

"Joseph said to them, 'Do not be afraid, for am I in the place of God?"
Genesis 50:19

INQUIRY–ACTION 15.1

THE LIFE OF JOSEPH

1. List the five most significant events in the life of Joseph.

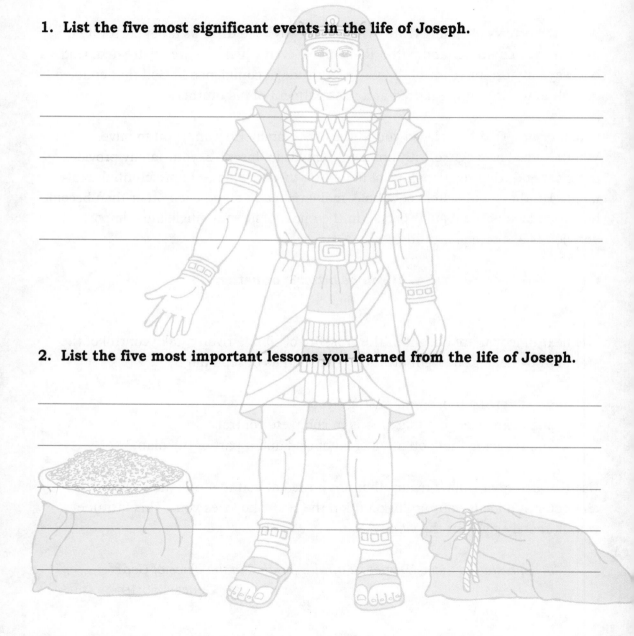

2. List the five most important lessons you learned from the life of Joseph.

INQUIRY-ACTION 15.2

PREFERENTIAL TREATMENT

Reality	*Perception*

INQUIRY-ACTION 15.2 (CONTINUED)

PREFERENTIAL TREATMENT

Lessons to Be Learned

INQUIRY-ACTION 15.3

THE PERSECUTED VS. THE PERSECUTORS

Reality	Perception

INQUIRY–ACTION 15.3 (CONTINUED)

THE PERSECUTED VS. THE PERSECUTORS

Lessons to Be Learned

INQUIRY-ACTION 15.4

**Work the puzzle to have a word bank for Genesis 50:20 and 45:7.
Use the words to write the verses on the next page.**

Across

1. good ___ gold
3. not out
6. super good
7. not after
9. in _____ to
11. conjunction, like and
12. determiner, like the
13. not my
14. future family
16. existences
17. rescue
20. not you
21. keep
22. not night
24. not from
25. not for
27. not bad
28. our planet
29. very bad

Down

1. around
2. made to go
3. pronoun—thing
4. persons
5. a saving from danger
8. not against
10. _____ and that
11. close, near
12. not dead
13. not me
15. not few
18. present tense—to be
19. to carry
20. intended
23. conjunction—2 or more
24. determiner, like a
26. Father in Heaven

INQUIRY–ACTION 15.4 (CONTINUED)

Genesis 50:20

_____

_____

_____

_____

_____

_____

Genesis 45:7

_____

_____

_____

_____

_____

PETER

Surviving Inconsistency

Trivia means little bits of unessential information. Are you ready for a little piece of trivia? You blink 25 times every minute. Each blink takes you about one-fifth of a second. Therefore, if you take a ten-hour automobile trip, averaging 60 miles per hour, your driver will speed along 30 miles with his eyes closed!

At the same rate of calculation, your eyes are closed for a total of 80 minutes during a 16-hour waking day! (If you're ambitious, compute the number of minutes your eyes are closed during an average lifetime.)

Isn't it amazing that we can go through an entire day, with our eyes closed for 80 minutes, and still be alive? God has created us in such a wonderful way that He has provided the rest our eyes need while allowing us to carry on our daily activities uninterrupted.

But the real lessons about the "eyes" and "seeing" are spiritual in nature. Our Lord frequently used common events to teach spiritual lessons. A good example is found in Mark 6.

Do you remember how Jesus fed thousands of people with a few loaves and fish? Immediately after that miracle, the disciples entered a boat and sailed toward the middle of the sea. Meanwhile Jesus sent the multitudes away and found a quiet place to pray. A sudden storm caused the disciples to panic. Without hesitation, Jesus came to their rescue walking across the sea.

Mark spoke of the disciples, ". . . And they were greatly amazed in themselves beyond measure, and marveled. For they had not understood about the loaves, because their heart was hardened" (verses 51–52). Jesus had already demonstrated His power with the miracle of the loaves and fish. The disciples had witnessed it, but just a few hours later they were paralyzed by fear. The reason? Their hearts were hardened.

The disciples suffered from spiritual nearsightedness. They had seen Jesus perform countless miracles, but still lacked the faith to trust Him when they faced difficulties. Although they had been specifically chosen by Jesus and had experienced His teaching and power, they were still spiritually immature.

Of all of the disciples, Peter is the one most remembered for his spiritual immaturity. His life is a case study in inconsistency. Frequently he spoke before thinking. He could rashly react in anger. He was often argumentative. When Jesus washed the feet of His disciples, Peter protested. Later he changed his mind and wanted to be washed all over after Jesus said, "If I do not wash you, you have no part with Me" (John 13:8).

Peter's inconsistent behavior is clearly illustrated in the end of our first story, which is also found in Matthew 14:24–31. When Peter saw Jesus walking on the water, he said "Lord, if it is You, command me to come to You on the water." Peter stepped out of the boat and began walking to Jesus. Taking his eyes off Jesus, he started to sink. "And immediately Jesus stretched out His hand and caught him, and said to him, 'O you of little faith, why did you doubt?'"

Probably the most well-known story of Peter's inconsistencies occurs in Luke 22:31–62. As the Lord approached the day of crucifixion, He told the disciples that one of them would deny Him. Peter quickly responded that he would never deny the Lord. Jesus then replied, "I tell you, Peter, the rooster shall not crow this day before you will deny three times that you know Me."

In the next few hours, three different individuals testified that they had seen Peter with Jesus. On each occasion, Peter denied that he knew Jesus. Following his third denial, Peter heard the rooster crowing and remembered the words of Jesus. Verse 62 says, "So Peter went out and wept bitterly."

This was probably one of the most difficult spiritual lessons that Peter ever experienced. However, it was a lesson he had to learn in order to overcome spiritual immaturity. Instead of inconsistent ups and downs, he had to develop spiritual maturity involving a strong, consistent direction that enabled him to maintain self-control, accept responsibility and behave according to his beliefs. Your need is the same as Peter's—to overcome the inconsistencies of life.

Inconsistencies are characteristic of the teen or "in-between" years from childhood to adulthood. You have two challenges before you. First, every person who is conscientious in his or her walk with the Lord realizes the importance of bringing every thought and action under the control of the Holy Spirit. In Peter's case, the process seems to have taken a lifetime. Maybe you face the same struggles. It seems that someone is always saying, "Grow up!" The good news is: you can and will! You may just have to work harder than others.

The other good news is: God can use you regardless of the mistakes of the past. Have you ever wondered how Peter could bear facing the Lord after denying Him three times? How could he ever go on with life? But his mistake was not fatal. Yours won't be either. You can always come back! You can still have a wonderful life of service to the Lord.

How good is your eyesight? Do you wear glasses or contacts, or do you have perfect vision without them? Matthew 6:22–23 says, "The lamp of the body is the eye. If therefore your eye is good, your whole body will be full of light. But if your eye is bad, your whole body will be full of darkness." As you have probably already realized, Jesus was not just talking about physical eyesight. He was more concerned about spiritual eyesight—the ability to know and understand the things of God. He was talking about the difference between spiritual immaturity and spiritual maturity.

To overcome inconsistencies, you must strengthen your spiritual eyesight; you need the light of God's Word and presence. When you started your day today, what light did you seek?

- Did you begin your day by seeking God's guidance either through reading His Word or through prayer?

- Did you determine to be His partner so that you would not do or say anything that would dishonor Him?

- When you thought about your blessings and all you planned to do today, did you thank the Lord for giving you life, health and ability?

God desires that you mature in your relationship with Him. Peter, in his later life, gave us great advice on how to do it.

"But grow in the grace and knowledge of our Lord and Savior Jesus Christ" (2 Peter 3:18).

"But may the God of all grace, who called us to His eternal glory by Christ Jesus, after you have suffered a while, perfect, establish, strengthen, and settle you. To Him be the glory and the dominion forever and ever. Amen" (1 Peter 5:10–11).

INQUIRY-ACTION 16.1

THE UPS AND DOWNS OF PETER

Place an arrow in each circle to indicate whether the response was positive or negative.

↑ Matthew 4:18–20	↓ ↑ John 21:3
↑ Luke 5:10–11	↑ John 21:17
↓ Matthew 14:29–31	↑ Acts 1:13–14
↑ Matthew 16:16–18	↑ Acts 2:14, 37–38
↓ Mark 8:32–33	↑ Acts 3:6–7
↑ John 6:66–69	↑ Acts 4:8–13
↓ ↑ Matthew 17:3–4	↑ Acts 4:19–20
↓ John 13:8–9	↑ Acts 9:39–40
↑ ↓ John 13:37–38	↑ Acts 10:44–45
↓ Mark 14:33, 37	↑ Acts 12:7–11
↓ John 18:10–11	↓ Galatians 2:11–14
↓ Luke 22:54–62	↑ Acts 15:6–11
↑ Luke 24:11–12	↑ ↓ 1 Peter 5:12

INQUIRY-ACTION 16.2

1 PETER 1:3-9

Blessed be the God and Father of our Lord Jesus Christ, who according to His abundant mercy has begotten us again to a living hope through the resurrection of Jesus Christ from the dead, to an inheritance incorruptible and undefiled and that does not fade away, reserved in heaven for you, who are kept by the power of God through faith for salvation ready to be revealed in the last time.

In this you greatly rejoice, though now for a little while, if need be, you have been grieved by various trials, that the genuineness of your faith, being much more precious than gold that perishes, though it is tested by fire, may be found to praise, honor, and glory at the revelation of Jesus Christ, whom having not seen, you love. Though now you do not see Him, yet believing, you rejoice with joy inexpressible and full of glory, receiving the end of your faith—the salvation of your souls.

INQUIRY-ACTION 16.3

PETER'S PRINCIPLES ON SUFFERING

1. _____
_____
_____
_____

2. _____
_____
_____
_____

3. _____
_____
_____

4. _____
_____
_____

INQUIRY-ACTION 16.4

PETER'S PRINCIPLES ON BEING CONSISTENT

1. _____

   _____

   _____

   _____

2. _____

   _____

   _____

   _____

3. _____

   _____

   _____

   _____

4. _____

   _____

   _____

   _____

Inquiry-Action 16.5

Sort it Out — *1 Peter 5:10–11*

Cross out the extra vowels to have a word bank that will help you write
the verses. Circle all the words you can find. They can be proper names
or any words found in a standard dictionary. See who can find the most.

abeautomiayoutheegoideaofallegoreaicewe
ehoocaulieeliedustoahaiuseatearunaileglrey
eoboeyechoirisetjosouisafeatearyeaouheave
suifofeareadawehaileperifecoateasetieable
ishoeastoreinagatehenoandeseatotealoeyeou
teaohueiamobeeiotahueagleeorayeaundothe
adominoioaneofourevereanodueverae

Did you find revere, domino or Andes? What about leis, eagle or agate?

ISAIAH

Surviving Uncertainties of Life

Do you believe that some things happen just by chance? Would you consider your-self lucky? unlucky? Do you have that feeling that "what will be, will be"? Or do you believe that things happen by design? Before you answer these questions, con-sider the following illustration from Dr. A Cressy Morrison, former president of the New York Academy of Sciences.

Let's suppose I take ten pennies, mark them 1 to 10, and then ask you to put them in your pocket. Next, I would ask you to shake your pocket so that the coins are totally mixed. I would then proclaim (with absolute confidence!) that I was going to reach into your pocket and pull out penny number 1. My chance of doing this successfully would be 1 in 10. Of course, if I did pull out penny number 1 you would be quite impressed.

Now, let's take the next step. I would put penny number 1 back into your pocket and have you shake the pennies again. Now, I would say, "I'm going to draw out penny number 2." My chances, this time, are not as great. As a matter of fact, the odds are 1 in 100. If I were to draw out number 3 next, the chances would be 1 in 1,000. If I use the same process and draw out each number in successive order, the odds of accomplishing all ten in successive order would be 1 in 10 billion.

Let's suppose that I accomplished this feat. You would immediately say, "No fair, you cheated." And you'd be right. The only way I could beat the odds would be to "fix" the game.

Think back to the opening paragraph of this chapter. Do the events of life happen by chance or by design? From the majesty of the universe to the infinite structure of the atom, design is evident. There is a Designer—God—and He is in complete control.

Every man, woman and child has struggled to understand why certain things happen in their lives. Right now, you probably are concerned about something in your life or in the life of a family member. Maybe it isn't really serious yet. Or maybe it is already at the point of crisis. Don't panic, and don't be afraid. Our God is in complete control of the situation.

That was the message of Isaiah to the people of Judah. Knowing the terrible hardships that the people would soon experience, Isaiah reminded them that God was in control. They did not need to be afraid. He would restore the nation to greatness.

Of course, that was the message at the end of the book of Isaiah. Read on, and you will learn the beginning of the story.

From the time of Abraham, God chose the nation of Israel to be the family of the Messiah—Christ, our Lord. Consequently, God's plan was to preserve and purify this nation for His purpose. For centuries, God had made it clear that His people were to keep themselves holy. They were not to worship false idols, and they were not to marry those who did not know the God of Israel. As you know, the people of Israel sinned against God on many occasions. The Old Testament is filled with examples of their disobedience.

Shortly after the death of Solomon, the nation of Israel divided into the northern and southern kingdoms. The northern kingdom was known as Israel, and the southern kingdom was known as Judah. The division occurred because of jealousy among the twelve tribes. Ten of the tribes formed the northern kingdom, while the remaining two tribes became the southern kingdom.

Isaiah was God's messenger to Judah. It was his task to tell the people that God was tired of their sin and mockery of His commandments. Isaiah was to announce that the time of punishment had come. Judah would be conquered by Babylon and taken captive. The nation would be in bondage to Babylon for 70 years. God would not be mocked. Sin had to be punished.

Isaiah knew that this message of impending doom would be devastating to Judah. They had never been taken captive by another nation. How would they respond? Could Isaiah give them any hope?

In the latter part of the book of Isaiah, God gives the prophet words of hope for the nation. Just as God would deliver them into the hands of the Babylonians, He would one day deliver them from captivity. Judah would once again experience greatness and honor among the nations. God was in complete control of the situation. He brought the punishment, and He would bring the restoration.

Isaiah's message is an important one for us today. First of all, we need to remember that God will not "look the other way" when we sin. He did not do it for Judah, and He will not do it for us. He will punish our sin. Paul reminds us in Romans 6:23 that ". . . the wages of sin is death . . . ." However, God also desires to restore us. In the same verse we are told ". . . but the gift of God is eternal life in Jesus Christ our Lord."

The second important lesson we learn from Isaiah is that God is in complete control. BECAUSE GOD IS IN CONTROL, WE CAN HAVE COMPLETE CONFIDENCE! If you believe that statement, it will change your life.

There is no doubt that you have already experienced some difficult times in your life. It could be a death in the family, parents' divorce, a serious illness or a variety of other personal issues. Unfortunately, you will experience many other difficulties throughout life.

Don't be depressed, REJOICE! Each of these "storms of life" will give you the opportunity to increase your trust in the Lord. If that surprises you, listen to the following:

Moses reminded Israel that when they faced difficult times, God would give them guidance. "When you are in distress, and all these things come upon you in the latter days, when you turn to the Lord your God and obey His voice (for the Lord your God is a merciful God), He will not forsake you nor destroy you" (Deuteronomy 4:30–31).

David also knew that he could have confidence because God was his strength. Throughout the book of Psalms, David taught this important principle to the nation of Israel. "God is our refuge and strength, a very present help in trouble" (Psalm 46:1).

Throughout his ministry, Paul had confidence because he knew that God was in complete control. "For I am persuaded that neither death nor life, nor angels nor principalities nor powers, nor things present nor things to come, nor height nor depth, nor any other created thing, shall be able to separate us from the love of God which is in Christ Jesus our Lord" (Romans 8:38–39).

The next time you face one of life's problems, or feel like nothing is ever going to go right; remind yourself that God is in complete control. When difficult times come, remember the five "nothings" of life:

◆ *Nothing can ever happen in your life that will take God by surprise.*

◆ *Nothing is so secret that God does not already know it.*

◆ *Nothing is so terrible that you cannot bring it to God in prayer.*

◆ *Nothing you face is too hard for God.*

◆ *Nothing will ever separate you from the love of God.*

Jesus wants us to experience comfort and confidence. That's why He said in John 16:33, "These things I have spoken unto you, that in Me you may have peace. In the world you will have tribulation; but be of good cheer, I have overcome the world." Rejoice! Our God is in complete control.

INQUIRY-ACTION 17.1

THE FIVE NOTHINGS OF LIFE

✦ *Nothing can ever happen in your life that will take God by surprise.*

✦ *Nothing is so secret that God does not already know it.*

✦ *Nothing is so terrible that you can not bring it to God in prayer.*

✦ *Nothing you face is too hard for God.*

✦ *Nothing will ever separate you from the love of God.*

INQUIRY-ACTION 17.2

ISAIAH'S REFERENCES TO THE NEW TESTAMENT

Isaiah	New Testament	Topic
7:14	Matthew 1:23	
9:1–2	Matthew 4:13–16	
9:6	Luke 2:7	
11:1–3	Luke 2:52; 3:21–22	
40:3–5	Luke 3:4–6	
35:5–6	Matthew 11:4–5	
40:11	John 10:14–17	
45:22	John 8:12	
55:1	John 7:37–38	
35:8	John 14:6	
9:7; 57:15–19	John 14:27	
61:1–2	Luke 4:16–21	

INQUIRY-ACTION 17.2 (CONTINUED)

ISAIAH'S REFERENCES TO THE NEW TESTAMENT

Isaiah	New Testament	Topic
5:1–5, 7	Matthew 21:33–34	
40:6–8	1 Peter 1:24–25	
56:7	Matthew 21:13	
42:1; 52:13	Matthew 12:17–21	
53:3, 7	John 1:29	
53:4–6	1 Peter 2:22–25	
26:1–19	Matthew 24:31	
50:6; 52:14	Matthew 27:30–31	
40:4–5	Revelation 1:7	
34:1–10; 63:1–6	Matthew 24:21–30	
61:10	Revelation 19:7–9	
11:9; 66:22–25	Revelation 21:1–4	

INQUIRY-ACTION 17.3

REASONS I CAN HAVE CONFIDENCE

If I trust God when facing uncertainties, He will give me . . .

INQUIRY-ACTION 17.4

ISAIAH 40:28–31

Write the verses using the synonyms as a help.

_____ _____ _____ _____?
　　　　　　　　　2nd person　　　　negative　　　understood, learned

_____ _____ _____ _____?
　　　　　　　　　2nd person　　　　negative　　　listened to

_____ _____ _____, _____ _____,
　　　eternal　　　　　Jehovah　　　　　　　　　Ruler of all

_____ _____ _____ _____ _____ _____ _____,
　maker　　　　　　　　　extent, all　　　　　　　　　this planet

_____ _____ _____ _____ _____ .
never　　weakly slumps　　　or　　　　tired, worn out

_____ _____ _____ _____ .
God's　　knowledge, wisdom　　　　not comprehended

_____ _____ _____ _____ _____
God　　　provides　　　strength, stability

_____, _____ _____ _____ _____ _____
fearful　　plus　　　　people　　　that　　possess

_____ _____ _____ _____ _____ .
zero　　strength, power　　God　　makes greater, adds　　power, ability

(Continued)

189

INQUIRY-ACTION 17.4 (CONTINUED)

_____ _____ _____ _____

also   young people   will

_____ _____ _____ _____ , _____

be weak, pass out   plus   tired, exhausted   plus

_____ _____ _____ _____

early age   people, males   will

_____ _____ , _____

completely   fail, be destroyed   in contrast

_____ _____ _____ _____ _____ _____

people   that   take time, are patient with   Ruler of all

_____ _____ _____ _____ ;

will   make new again, regain   people's   power, ability

_____ _____ _____ _____ _____

people   will   rise with sureness   having   arms of birds

_____ _____ , _____ _____ _____

the same as   strong, majestic fowls   people   will   race, jog

_____ _____ _____ _____ , _____ _____

plus   negative   tired, worn out   people   will

_____ _____ _____ _____ .

stride, pace   plus   negative   weakly slump, pass out

REVIEW

Butterflies. They are beautiful and yet so delicate. On a warm and sunny day, you will see them wherever you find fields of grass and flowers. Their colors and designs are absolutely magnificent. They are a unique part of God's creation.

People have always been fascinated by butterflies. When John was little, he used to try to get as close to a butterfly as possible. Silently, he would observe their habits and the beautiful designs on their wings. In his mind, butterflies were the most beautiful and fragile of all the creatures God had made.

Many years later, John was a grown man with a family of his own. While walking in the neighborhood one day, he spied a cocoon lying along the side of the path. Somehow the twig had been knocked from the tree and the cocoon had survived undamaged, still woven to the branch.

The memories of his childhood returned. As he had done many years before, he picked up the cocoon and gently protected it by wrapping it in his handkerchief. At home, he found a wide-top Mason jar and punched holes in the lid. Like he had done as a child, he placed the cocoon in the jar for easy viewing and protection. He knew that their cat, affectionately known as "Troublemaker," would love to get his paws on the cocoon. So, John placed the jar on the fireplace mantel.

Over the next couple of days, John carefully watched the activity in the cocoon. Although there wasn't much action at first, the cocoon's movement increased as each day passed. He watched more closely and saw the cocoon trembling with activity. Nothing else happened. The cocoon remained tightly glued to the twig, and there was no sign of wings.

Finally the shaking became so intense that John thought the butterfly would die from the struggle. He removed the jar lid, took out his knife, and carefully made a tiny slit in the side of the cocoon. Almost immediately, one wing appeared and then out stretched the other. The butterfly was free!

The butterfly seemed to enjoy its freedom as it walked along the mantel. John knew the butterfly would spread its wings and fly away at any moment. He patiently waited . . . and waited . . . and waited. But it didn't fly.

Not knowing what to think, John called his neighbor who taught high school science. When he described how he had carefully made a small slit in the cocoon, the teacher stopped him.

"That's the reason he can't fly," he said. "The struggle is what gives the butterfly the strength to fly. Without the struggle to get out of the cocoon, the butterfly's wings do not mature properly."

This is a valuable lesson for each of us as we face challenges in life. Our maturity will come as we learn to "survive and thrive"—no matter what obstacles, or struggles, we may face.

Take a moment and carefully review the following list of "survival challenges" you studied this semester:

Surviving Temptation	Adam and Eve
Surviving Broken Relationships	Barnabas
Surviving Poor Decisions	Joshua
Surviving Rejection	Leah
Surviving Peer Pressure	Nehemiah
Surviving Family Stress	Mary
Surviving Lack of Confidence	Timothy
Surviving an Unknown Future	Abraham
Surviving Loss of Self-Control	Absalom
Surviving a Terrible Loss	Ruth
Surviving Sin's Consequences	David
Surviving Irresponsible Behavior	Samson
Surviving Personal Conflicts	Philemon

As you reviewed the list, did you realize that you are struggling with at least one of these challenges right now? If so, go back to that chapter and review the principles of "surviving and thriving" contained there. Just like the butterfly, you will only be successful as you personally work your way through the struggle you are facing.

As we bring this semester's study to a close, remember, **"You are important to God!"** You are like Emily in the play, "Our Town," who lists her address as:

Grovers Corner
New Hampshire
United States of America
Western Hemisphere
Planet Earth
Solar System
The Universe
Mind of God

Inside the mind of God . . . that is about as important a place as you can be. The next time you face problems, lack confidence or feel all alone, remember that you are important to Him. You are so important that He sent His Son, Jesus Christ, to die for you. "For God so loved the world that He gave His only begotten Son, that whoever believes in Him should not perish, but have everlasting life" (John 3:16).

You can face the future, and survive any challenge, if you are living by faith and in the strength that God can provide. Commit the following verse to memory as a reminder of the strength that God provides to help you "survive and thrive."

"The Lord is my strength and my shield; my heart trusted in Him, and I am helped; therefore my heart greatly rejoices, and with my song I will praise Him." (Psalm 28:7)

INQUIRY-ACTION 18.1

REVIEW IT OR LOSE IT

Bible Character: _____

Summary of Life: _____

_____

_____

Challenge/s faced by the character:

_____

_____

Three important principles I have learned about surviving and thriving when facing this challenge:

    1) _____

    2) _____

    3) _____

The main reason students do not have success in facing this challenge:

_____

_____

Example of how I can survive and thrive in this challenge:

_____

_____

INQUIRY-ACTION 18.2

REVIEW IT OR LOSE IT

Bible Character: _____

Summary of Life: _____

_____

_____

Challenge/s faced by the character:

_____

_____

Three important principles I have learned about surviving and thriving when facing this challenge:

    1) _____

    2) _____

    3) _____

The main reason students do not have success in facing this challenge:

_____

_____

Example of how I can survive and thrive in this challenge:

_____

_____

Inquiry–Action 18.3

Final Commitment

Your paper will not be seen by anyone except you. Your honesty will allow God to work as you develop godly character.

✔ **The one truth from this course that has been most important to me is . . .**

_____

✔ **A challenge area which I feel confident in handling is . . .**

_____

✔ **The challenge area that needs most improvement in how I handle things is . . .**

_____

✔ **The biggest obstacle to my improving this area is . . .**

_____

✔ **Some things I want to work on are . . .**

_____

_____

✔ **I want to commit myself to developing godly character. Yes ☐   No ☐**
If yes, complete the next page.

INQUIRY–ACTION 18.4

Commitment to Successfully Facing the Challenges of Life

Based on the challenges presented in this course, I am willing to commit myself to the development of godly responses.

I understand that this includes my commitment to a right attitude and actions based on God's Word.

Signed: _____

Dated: _____

"The Lord is my strength and my shield; my heart trusted in Him, and I am helped; therefore my heart greatly rejoices, and with my song I will praise Him."
(Psalm 28:7)

GLOSSARY

GLOSSARY

acceptance – being included, belonging, feeling loved. (4)

anatomy – the internal structure, the pieces that fit together. (13)

aptitude – a natural ability that helps a person do something well. (9)

apology – saying that you are sorry and really meaning it. (2)

attitude – the mental or emotional mindset that is shown in outward behaviors. (9)

avoid – to stay away from as in "avoiding the appearance of evil." (1)

bitterness – internal anger, strong feelings of resentment and revenge; must be overcome with forgiveness. (4)

broken relationship – a separation from a friend or family member with whom you were once closely connected. (2)

challenge – to face a problem or difficulty that needs to be solved. (8)

commitment – a promise to God, self or someone important to you; a pledge that should not be broken. (9) (12)

confess – to admit your wrong, to agree with God that you sinned; to speak forth what is in your heart. (11)

confidence – a feeling of inner strength and ability; a sureness. We can have confidence because of our dependence on God. (7) (17)

conform – to change to fit a mold or expectation. We are not to be conformed to the world, but conformed to the image of Christ. (5)

conflict – different points of view that lead to broken relationships and hostility. (13)

consequences – the results of decisions or actions; related reactions or outcomes. (3) (12)

control – to rule or manage; to have authority or power to direct. (17)

GLOSSARY

coping – to manage life during tough times; to continue doing what's expected although upset or grieving. (10)

deceive – to trick, fool or lie to someone. (4)

decision – a choice made; a selection. All decisions have consequences. (3)

denial – pretending that something is not real or is not happening. Denial is one of the normal stages of grief. (10)

deny – to refuse to recognize; reject, unwilling to admit, declare untrue. (16)

duration – a measure of time; how long something lasts. (12)

emotional intelligence, or EQ – an emotional nature that allows a person to face problems, seek solutions, get along with others, not be overwhelmed and to bounce back quickly. Many people consider it more important for success than intelligence, or IQ. (Introduction)

enticement – invitation (to sin). (1)

evil – sinful, wrong, opposite to good and right; describes activities opposed to God and promoted by Satan. (1)

fair – just or equal treatment of all members of a group who share the same needs. When someone has special needs, being fair means to treat the person in accordance with his needs. (15)

faith – a strong belief that what God says is absolutely true; to act in confidence on that belief. (8)

faithfulness – the process of demonstrating faith; being dependable, being regular in attendance. (14)

family stress – occurs when events produce unexpected pressure on a family. (6)

fools – those who disregard God and live according to their own wants and pleasures. They ignore the consequences of their actions. (12)

GLOSSARY

forgive – to no longer remember or respond to another's wrong. In the same way God forgives us, we are obligated to forgive others. ((4) (11)

friend – a person, other than family, with whom you enjoy a positive relationship. (2)

grief – a deep sorrow or sadness that naturally happens when facing a terrible loss or tragedy. (10)

holy – pure, without sin; awesome heavenly presence that produces worship, repentance and service on our part. (17)

immature – a lack of normal maturity compared to others the same age. (16)

impute – to place debts on the account of another person. Our sins were imputed to Christ. (13)

inconsistency – not behaving in a logical or reliable manner. (16)

iniquity – sin, as in when you twist God's law through deception. (11)

injustices – things that are unfair or unjust such as mistreatment of another person. (15)

intensity – a measure of strength; a reference to how bad or how often an undesirable behavior occurs. (12)

irresponsible – to lack responsibility; to not consider consequences; to act without thinking, to disregard others, to be deceptive, etc. (12)

justified – to be made right with God "just as if I'd" never sinned. (13)

kinsman-redeemer – a close relative who was able to buy back land, marry a widow or pay the debts owed by someone in slavery. Boaz was a kinsman-redeemer for Ruth. Christ is a Kinsman-Redeemer for us. (10)

lineage – the family line, ancestors. Christ was of the house and lineage of David. (10)

loss – a terrible loss is a tragedy from which you are likely to have physical and emotional pain for most of your life. (10)

love – to seek the benefit of another even if it requires personal sacrifice; unconditional acceptance, emotional bonding. We love God because He first loved us. (4)

GLOSSARY

mature – fully developed in body, mind or spirit, as compared to others the same age. (16)

maturity – a characteristic that includes wisdom, strong personal values, good decision making and responsible actions. (5)

mentor – an older person who counsels and teaches you skills for life. (2)

mistreat – to act or speak in a wrong way toward someone. (15)

mockers – fools or scorners who make fun of God's words and ways. (12)

natural – related to nature or flesh; how we react based on our own feelings and desires. (4)

Nazirite – a person who made a promise or vow to not drink wine, not touch dead people or animals, and to not shave or cut hair. It was a sign that the person was dedicated (set apart) to God. (12)

overwhelming responsibility – assuming leadership or accountability to a level almost greater than you can bear. (14)

passions – strong desires that motivate a person to act; often used to describe sexual desires. (12)

peacemakers – people who seek resolution of conflicts and restore relationships. (13)

peer pressure – a strong push to fit in and gain approval from one's friends or age group. It can be both positive and negative. (5)

perception – understanding; insight; receipt of information through the senses. (15)

poor decision – one which clearly violates God's Word or chooses your way over God's way. (3)

posterity – the continuing line of a family in the future. (15)

preferential treatment – to show favoritism, to love one more than another. Jacob showed preferential treatment to Joseph in giving him a coat of many colors. (15)

pressure – stress arising from problems or difficulties; pushing in a direction—perhaps to do wrong. (6)

GLOSSARY

presumptuous – being prideful, focused only on self; to assume that you are more important or better than others. (15)

principle – a basic belief about what is important or how things work. (3)

probability – the likelihood a specific event or situation will occur, often expressed with a number; chance. (17)

providence – the oversight and management by God of the affairs of our lives. It is evidence of His power and sovereignty. (10)

rebellion – an overthrow of authority; a fight against government, parents and God. (9)

reconcile/reconciliation – to bring peace between two or more people. We are reconciled to God because of Christ's death on the cross. (17) (2)

relationship – two or more people who share a common concern, defined by time together, communication, shared values, a desire to see the best for the other person, etc. (2)

rejection – the opposite of acceptance and love; to exclude, turn away from. (4) (6)

repent – to confess and forsake sin; changing to the opposite direction. (11)

resilience – the ability to rebound after experiencing difficult challenges in life. (Introduction)

resist – to strive against, push away or avoid situations or people. We are to resist Satan and temptation. (1)

resolution – a solution to a problem or conflict; to bring things back together. (13)

responsible – describes a person who ably responds with excellence of character and actions; one who accepts the consequences of his decisions and actions, thinks ahead, regards others, does the right thing, can be depended on. (12)

responsibility – a job, chore or assignment which a person must complete, and potentially, give an account for; things you are expected to do, and if undone, there is a penalty. (14)

GLOSSARY

restoration – the process to renew or restore. When there is a broken relationship, we should seek restoration. (2) (11)

revenge – to get even, retaliate, hurting someone back, giving evil for evil. (4)

ridicule – to tease, criticize, make fun of, embarrass, treat as a fool. (15)

righteous – being declared right before God because Christ paid for sin; being justified. (13)

scorners – fools and mockers; those who show contempt for God. (12)

self-confidence – a sense that you can depend on your feelings, thoughts and actions. It gives you assurance that you are capable of achieving what you want. (5)

self-control – the management of one's attitudes, speech and actions. It comes as a result of surrendering ourselves completely to the leading of the Holy Spirit. (9) (12)

sibling rivalry – the disagreements, both physical and verbal, that occur between brothers and sisters. (15)

sin – 1) to break God's law or standard; 2) to do less than God expects, as when a person knows to do good but fails to do it. (1) (11)

solicitation – an enticement or invitation, as in "temptation is a solicitation to do evil." (1)

sovereignty of God – the unlimited power God has to control the affairs of nature and history. (15) (17)

stress – difficulties of life that cause pressure; tension or forces that cause the body to react, sometimes in unhealthy ways. It can include eustress—a normal pressure that motivates to action, or distress—strong emotional upheaval. (Introduction)

strife – disagreements, arguments, differences of opinion that lead to broken relationships. (6)

supernatural – above nature or flesh; refers to what God does, not what man does. (4)

GLOSSARY

survive – to live through a difficult experience or a life-threatening situation.   (Introduction)

taunt – ridicule, mock, scoff. (15)

temptation – an enticement or invitation to sin, with the implied promise of benefit to be gained from choosing the path of disobedience. (1)

thrive – to overcome challenges in a way that you are more successful than ever before.   (Introduction)

timidity – a feeling of shyness, doubt, fear and unsureness. (7)

tragedy – a traumatic, terrible event such as an unexpected death in a family, diagnosis of a terminal illness, etc., that produces great emotional pain. (10)

transgress – to break the law; sin as in breaking God's law or failing to keep His commandments. (11)

trespass – to step over the boundary line; sin as in breaking the law. (11)

trust – to believe, to have faith, to totally depend on someone. God wants us to trust Him when facing difficult problems. (10)

U O ME – an acronym for "you owe me"; a sense that others have wronged you and should pay for it. To forgive means to give up the "U O ME's." (13)

uncertainties of life – the situations faced that are unsure in their outcome. With God we can face uncertainties knowing He protects and provides for us. (17)

unequally yoked – to have a close relationship, such as marriage or business partnership, in which the two people are very different in their beliefs and ways of life. It especially means a believer yoked to a nonbeliever, which is forbidden in 2 Corinthians 6:14. (12)

unknown future – the events of the future which are unknown and unpredictable today. (8)

way of life – direction and manner of living. We are challenged to choose God's way over our own natural way of life. (12)

PRESCRIPTIONS
FOR
LIFE CHALLENGES

PRESCRIPTIONS FOR LIFE'S CHALLENGES

> ## Surviving and Thriving
> Romans 8:18, 28, 31b, 35, 37
> Jeremiah 31:3 and 29:11

Broken Relationships
Colossians 3:12–14
Proverbs 17:17 and 18:24
Philippians 2:3–4

Family Stress
Colossians 3:18–21
Ephesians 5:21–22, 25; 6:1, 4
Romans 12:9–10
Luke 1:46–50

Inconsistency
1 Peter 5:10–11
Matthew 16:16–17
2 Peter 3:17–18
Matthew 26:41
2 Corinthians 12:10
Romans 8:13–14

Irresponsible Behavior
Psalm 37:3–5
Proverbs 10:8 and 14
Romans 14:17–19
2 Thessalonians 2:15–17

Lack of Confidence
2 Timothy 1:7
1 Timothy 4:12
Proverbs 3:25–26
Hebrews 13:5–6
1 Chronicles 28:20

Loss of Self-Control
Titus 2:11–13
1 Peter 1:13–15
Proverbs 25:28
Philippians 2:1–3

Overwhelming Responsibilities
2 Thessalonians 2:15–17
2 Timothy 2:15–16
Psalm 71:1
1 Corinthians 7:24

Peer Pressure
Proverbs 4:14–15 and 18–19
Ephesians 5:3–8
Romans 12:1–2
Proverbs 23:17–21

Personal Conflicts
Galatians 5:13–15
Philemon 3–5
James 1:17–18
John 15:14–15

Poor Decisions
Joshua 24:14–15, 24
Romans 12:1–2
Proverbs 3:5–6
Hebrews 11:24–26

Rejection
John 6:37 and 39
Colossians 3:12–17
Romans 15:5–7
Ephesians 1:5–6
Psalm 145:17–19

Sibling Rivalry
Genesis 50:20 and 45:7
1 Peter 3:8–9
Luke 6:30–31
Ephesians 4:31–32

Sin's Consequences
Psalm 51:10–12
Psalm 51:1–3
Psalm 32:1–2
Proverbs 28:13 and 29:1
Romans 8:1–2

Temptation
1 Corinthians 10:13
James 4:7–8
1 Peter 5:8–9
James 1:13–15
Matthew 26:41 or Mark 14:38

A Terrible Loss
Psalm 91:1–2
Ruth 1:16
Romans 8:38
Psalm 126:5–6
Colossians 1:13–14

Uncertainties of Life
Isaiah 40:28–31
Isaiah 41:10
Isaiah 6:8
Isaiah 7:14
Revelation 19:11–16

An Unknown Future
Hebrews 11:8, 10, 16
James 4:13–15
Genesis 12:1–3
Genesis 15:16
Galatians 3:6, 9
Romans 4:20–21

NOTES

He
1 Hello

Peter ↑ (+)	↓ (−)

Peter ↑ (+)

- eager
- quick to obey
- 1st among disciples
- inner circles of Christ
- motivated
- hard worker
- trusting

↓ (−)

- emotional
- impetuous
- busy
- hasty
- spoke w/o thinking
- explosive
- violent
- disloyal

12 Disciples

Simon Peter

Andrew

James - son of Zebedee

John

Philip

Bartholomew

Thomas

Matthew

James -- son of Alphaeus

Thaddues

Simon

Judas ✗

✗ Replaced in Acts 1

✗ Matihias

NOTES

NOTES

NOTES

NOTES

NOTES

NOTES